# Black Country
# MURDERS

# Black Country
# MURDERS

IAN M. BOTT

First published 2009

The History Press
The Mill, Brimscombe Port
Stroud, Gloucestershire, GL5 2QG
www.thehistorypress.co.uk

British Library Cataloguing in Publication Data.
A catalogue record for this book is available from the British Library.

ISBN 978 0 7509 5053 4

Typesetting and origination by The History Press
Printed in Great Britain by Henry Ling Limited, at the Dorset Press,
Dorchester, DT1 1HD

# CONTENTS

# ACKNOWLEDGEMENTS

This publication would have been impossible to produce without the expertise, support and kindness, from the most excellent and encouraging people that I have encountered during the punishing schedule experienced in researching and writing these pages.

Particular thanks must go to the sincere and dedicated staff of the three Local Authority Archive Services listed below, whose unstinting assistance has been invaluable.

Equal thanks is given to the excellent production team at The History Press for their professional guidance from start to finish in completing this daunting task.

My gratitude also lies with Katharine, Steven and Simon Dudley for very patiently electronically transcribing my handwritten drafts, very often at only a moment's notice.

Also, I must not forget my dear mother, Rita, who ensured that I was never short of ready meals, and more, when always short of time.

Finally, I would like to acknowledge all family, friends and colleagues alike, whose helpful comments and continued interest has been greatly appreciated, but in particular: J.C. Brown, Ron Davies, Dudley Archives and Local History Service, Katharine Dudley, Simon Dudley, Steven Dudley, Pat Dunn, Michael Glasson, Stan Hill, Bernard Minton, Nicola Morris, Michael Reuter, Sandwell Community History and Archive Services, Walsall Local History Centre, *Walsall Observer*.

# INTRODUCTION

We go about our daily lives, working, shopping, walking and relaxing in the most unassuming of places, often blissfully unaware of the darker secrets, lost to time, of our housing estates, town centres and public open spaces, wherever we may reside.

This is the conclusion I have reached, after countless hours of research into these ten horrific Black Country murder cases, two of which being triple murders, resulting in the untimely deaths of fourteen tragic victims, including six innocent and defenceless young children.

Such ordinary everyday locations, which in their time have become the stage where some of the region's more gruesome crimes have been enacted, include a well-known public park, a busy town centre estate agents, a semi-detached 1930s council house, and an environmentally-friendly waste recycling plant.

The true-life dramas contained in this volume have been specially chosen in the hope that they are largely unfamiliar to the reader, and so make more gripping and knife-edge stories for the connoisseur of the Black Country's darker side. Everyone will have heard before about such famous cases as 'Bella in the Wych Elm', therefore no already well-known murder features in this book.

Collectively spanning the years 1900-1958, each chilling tale has been carefully researched using, amongst other sources, contemporary newspaper reports, capturing the full revulsion and sensationalism experienced by our Black Country ancestors, some of whom undoubtedly will have had their eyewitness accounts passed on through successive family generations, while other such reminisces may, over time, have faded to mere hearsay or been completely forgotten.

For the genealogist, no person who was mentioned in the original reports, no matter how small their role in the events, has been omitted from these pages, their names being indexed alongside those of court officials and magistrates at the rear of the book. Exact addresses are only given in cases where the original buildings have been long demolished, so as not to disturb or offend those who may presently reside in premises which once bore witness to tragic events of human suffering.

Black Country folk will be familiar with the occupational situations of both victims and perpetrators alike. The traditional industries of brick making, iron founding, plus lock and keysmiths are but some which feature in each story, in one case the workplace being the actual scene of the crime. Older locals will also be familiar with some of the living conditions described, often poverty-stricken nineteenth-century slums, which were hastily erected to accommodate the population explosion as migrant workers settled in the region during its industrial heyday.

Such conditions today would very probably be accepted as mitigating circumstances in defence of a criminal act, but back in those days, when the class divide was much greater, poverty was an everyday part of life tolerated by our Black Country ancestors.

Motives for these fourteen killings range from theft, revenge, passion and sexual infatuation, though when brought to book, and with the prospect of the death sentence hanging over them, many of those charged chose to pursue insanity as a line of defence.

Of the ten killers here, all of them men, six were handed down the sentence of death although only half of that number actually swung on the gallows, the other three being reprieved and their sentences being commuted to terms of penal servitude.

Some may argue that not all the killers named within these pages were convicted of murder, instead being found guilty of the lesser charge of manslaughter. I will answer that; call it what you may, for the poor victim there is only one outcome; that being unlawful death at the hands of another.

Ian M. Bott
Wednesbury, 2009

# 1

# OUTRAGE ON THE HILLY-PIECE

*West Bromwich, 1900*

Halfway between Carters Green, West Bromwich, and Holloway Bank, Wednesbury, the great London to Holyhead coach road passes through a residential district known as Hill Top. Once an ancient rural settlement, by the year 1900 its vestiges of green pasture were scarred with abandoned colliery workings or sprawling ironworks. Here, the close-knit community was made up of shopkeepers and wealthy residents in their spacious villas lining the highway alongside the newly built library and police station, whilst its poorer inhabitants lived their hardworking lives in cramped terraces, tucked away in the side streets. One such quarter was Rydding Square, originally called Long Square by way of its straight and narrow layout, which terminated on the waste ground of the abandoned Wallface Colliery. This slum-standard early nineteenth-century development lay along Witton Lane, which links the Hateley Heath district with Hill Top, just below the parish church of St James.

Mrs Louisa Coleyshaw, who the press later described as 'a woman of the poorer working class', was staying up for the return of her eldest daughter, Rebecca, from her employment at the Junction Inn, Witton Lane, late in the evening of Monday 26 November 1900, at the family home, No. 35 Rydding Square. When she had not arrived by 11 p.m., her younger sister, Matilda, aged nine, was summoned to go to the top of the entry to look out for her. It was raining heavily that night, so the little girl, dressed in a striped flannel skirt, covered her head with a white shawl and set off out into the night.

About twenty minutes later, Rebecca entered the house alone having not encountered Matilda, so she, in turn, was sent out to search for her sibling.

Rebecca returned a further fifteen minutes later saying that she had made no sighting of Matilda. A young neighbour named Thomas Cooper was sent to a nearby aunt's of the girl, but came back with the message that Matilda was not there. Louisa informed her husband that their child was missing but told him she could manage the search alone and not to get up. He had retired to bed earlier that night in charge of their third daughter, still an infant. Louisa then stayed up all night making enquiries with neighbours and trudged the rain-lashed streets calling out for her girl.

Meanwhile, a short distance away at No. 67 Witton Lane, Thomas Harvey was another person waiting up that night. He was anticipating the return of his son-in-law, Joseph Lowe, a twenty-eight-year-old widower, who was unexpectedly late in returning from an evening out to the Bird in Hand public house, situated in Queen Street which lay between Hawkes Lane and Castle Street, to the west of the old coach road. At two minutes to midnight, Lowe, a shingler at a local foundry, entered through the front door of the house where he lodged together with his three-year-old son and Mr Harvey, his wife, Mary-Ann, and their daughter, Louisa, aged nineteen. His clothing soaked through, Lowe acknowledged his father-in-law with 'How do you do', then walked straight through the passage that led to the kitchen and parlour where he removed his wet jacket. He shortly returned to the front room where he lit his pipe and then went out into the backyard to smoke it. A few minutes later, he returned inside, wished Mr Harvey 'Goodnight' and then made his way up to bed without another word.

The following morning at 9 a.m., Tuesday 27 November, Charles Piggott, a thirty-three-year-old farm bailiff working for the Patent Shaft & Axletree Co., had left his home at No. 1 Holloway Bank, to walk his rounds at Ball's Hill Field, which was known locally as the 'Hilly-Piece'. This was a large tract of surviving pasture belonging to Ball's Hill Farm, it was bounded by Holloway Bank, Witton Lane and Crookhay Lane, the latter originally joining with Witton Lane at the side of the Junction Inn. Here a rough footpath crossed over a set of wooden stiles and took a short cut over the field back to Holloway Bank. At this end, another track led to the abandoned Ball's Hill Colliery and was known as the 'Colliery Road' (today's Hampshire Road). From here, about 60yds into the field from the boundary fence, close to a bush, Piggott made a horrific discovery. The pitiful body of little Matilda Coleyshaw lay face down in the mud, her striped flannel skirt missing and her remaining underclothes disarranged. She was quite dead. Immediately, he made his way to Hill Top police station, were Sergeant John Owen, a native of Montgomery, resided with his wife and daughter in the adjoining sergeant's house. Together they returned to the Hilly-Piece where Sergeant Owen first examined the surrounding ground, but could find no signs of a struggle or any footprints, although it had rained continually nearly all night long.

On turning over the body, he noticed bloodstains on the ground beneath where she lay. These and more on her arms seemed to have originated from a wound in her trunk. Her arms were bent at the elbows and her hands half closed. He observed that her head was quite bare and that the sodden white shawl lay alongside. Sergeant Owen removed the body to the district mortuary where he took charge of the child's clothing for later forensic examination. During the post-mortem carried out by medical officer Dr W.H. Plummer, it was recorded that the child was 3ft 10in in height and was well nourished. It was his opinion that undoubtedly she was the victim of rape, and that death had ensued almost immediately after the offence had taken place. He concluded that the cause of death was suffocation, after being 'outraged with extreme violence'.

Earlier the same morning, at about 5 a.m., Mary-Ann Harvey arose from bed and set about her chores. On entering the parlour, she noticed that Lowe's jacket was folded inside-out and laid upon a chair. Being a tidy person, she placed it over her arm to hang up, but noticed that it was still saturated with rainwater, so put it back where she found it, to dry, and went about her housework. At 9.30 a.m., Lowe came downstairs and straight away went out into the backyard. His sister-in-law, Louisa, was out in the garden, but they did not speak. A while later, he returned to the house and sat down to breakfast. Mrs Harvey noticed that he was wearing the same trousers as the night before, wet and muddy as they were. She could see that Lowe had attempted to remove some stains from them, arousing her suspicions. With this in mind, she went back to the parlour to take a closer look at the jacket, but was surprised to find that it had been removed.

Later in the morning after Lowe had left the house, Mrs Harvey voiced her suspicions to her daughter and together, they decided to go upstairs and make a search of Lowe's bedroom, located to the front of the house. Inside a tin trunk at the side of this bed, they found the still wet jacket folded up on top of his waistcoat, which had also been worn the night before. The jacket sleeves were quite muddy, but more sinister were about three spots of blood on the right-hand cuff. On close examination, the waistcoat also revealed a bloodstain. The two women folded the two items of clothing back up and replaced them carefully in the trunk where they had been found. They went back downstairs where they discussed their find and what they should do.

Meanwhile news of the horrific discovery of poor Matilda Coleyshaw's abused body spread like wildfire throughout the Hill Top district and beyond. On learning this, Mary-Ann and Louisa decided upon confronting Lowe about his suspicious actions.

At 2 p.m. on Wednesday 28 November, Lowe, who had worked a night shift, arrived at the Harvey household and took a seat in the front living room. Mrs Harvey surprised him by asking 'Why did you put your jacket up all for wet?' He replied that he had fetched it out of the trunk to dry and then put it back. Mrs Harvey continued 'Joe, you wasn't in a bother or a scramble? Only there is blood on the right cuff of your jacket sleeve, a very little but not much.' Lowe said nothing but just laughed. When pressed, he explained that about ten days earlier, he had slaughtered a duck with a knife whilst wearing the same clothing. He reared ducks and fowl in the back garden.

Unsatisfied with his answers, Louisa then took over the grilling asking, 'Where were you, Joe, on Monday night?.'

He replied, 'Me? At Bromwich.' The conversation continued.

'What were you doing?' Louisa asked.

'Nothing.'

'Wasn't you fighting?' persisted Louisa.

'No!' insisted Lowe.

'Well there's some blood on your jacket cuff, where did you get it from?'

'There isn't.' said Lowe.

'I've seen some.' persisted Louisa.

Lowe left the room and returned seconds later with the jacket. When the bloodspots were pointed out to him, he cried 'God's truth, if it ain't a hot 'un! Call me up at half past four, I'm going to bed.' With that, he left the two women and made his way upstairs to his room.

One and a half hours later, the Harveys received a knock at the front door. It was Sergeant Owen, accompanied with colleagues Sergeant Wilson and Detective Constable Heappy, who were carrying out house-to-house enquiries. During a short conversation, the Harvey women's suspicions came to the fore. From what they were told, the three officers decided they must speak to Lowe urgently, so made their way upstairs and entered his bedroom. There, he was found to be sound asleep. Detective Constable Heappy walked to the side of the bed and woke him up. He asked 'Are you Joseph Lowe?' to which Lowe replied 'Yes'. Heappy then snapped, 'Get up'. Lowe raised himself up in bed. He was still wearing the same shirt he had worn on the Monday night. Heappy observed 'You have got blood on your shirt wristband.'

'It is off my chin. I've worn it three weeks,' Lowe replied.

Heappy continued, ' You are about to be arrested on a charge of causing the death of a little girl on Monday night last and whatever you say will be used in evidence against you. Do you understand the gravity of the charge?'

'Yes,' Lowe replied. Heappy then opened the tin trunk and took from it the jacket and waistcoat which he showed to Lowe. 'Them are what I had on and these are the trousers that I was wearing.' Lowe said, pointing to the pair he had just pulled on.

Sergeant Owen took the jacket downstairs accompanied by Detective Constable Heappy, leaving Sergeant Wilson in charge of Lowe. Whilst they were alone, Lowe asked Wilson, 'Is the sergeant going to lock me up?' to which Wilson replied 'Yes'. Lowe then said 'I'll tell you, I never saw the girl. I was in Jack Hawthorne's, the Bird in Hand until 11 o'clock that night and when I left, I went up Queen Street and round by the clock tower (at Carters Green) and back down Witton Lane. I went home and went to bed. No one saw me in the Hilly-Piece that night.' If Lowe was innocent, he had certainly learned where the body was found.

Meanwhile downstairs, Louisa Harvey suggested that the jacket's pockets be searched. In one, Sergeant Owen found a silk handkerchief which appeared to be bloodstained. The two officers returned upstairs where Lowe was shown the soiled item. Owen said 'I have found this in your jacket pocket and there is blood on it.' Lowe explained 'It is mine, I had it that night. I don't know how the blood got on it.' Lowe was then arrested and put into custody at West Bromwich Central police station in the High Street. There, Sergeant Owen told him 'You will be charged with causing the death of Matilda Coleyshaw at Hill Top, West Bromwich on Monday 26 November 1900 and anything you say will be taken down and may be used in evidence against you. Lowe protested 'I never knew the wench. I never saw 'one' after I left Jack Hawthorne's.'

The inquest on the body of Matilda Coleyshaw was opened at West Bromwich by the borough coroner, Mr James Clark, on Wednesday 28 November. In addition to the evidence given concerning the disappearance of the little girl two days earlier and the discovery of her pitiful body the following day, the coroner also attached interest to the finding of another body nearby which excited local gossips to draw a hasty conclusion. A local reservist named Jones had committed suicide on the Great Western rail line at Hill Top, leading to much speculation that he had maltreated the girl, being afterwards overcome with guilt. The coroner was quick to prove that the rumours were without foundation and, following Dr Plummer's post-mortem report, adjourned the inquest for a fortnight.

A large crowd congregated outside the West Bromwich Law Court on the morning of Friday 30 November when Joseph Lowe appeared before Mr J. Guest JP, charged on suspicion of causing the death of Matilda Coleyshaw. For the police, Chief Superintendent Whitehurst explained that during the course of their enquiries, Sergeants Owen and Wilson with Detective Constable Heappy had come across a soldier named Edward Ray Boffey who was on furlough (military leave) and had given them a statement to the effect that he had spoken to Lowe in Witton Lane at about 11.15 p.m. on the night of the murder. This contradicted Lowe's statement to the police that at that very hour, he was making his way towards the clock tower at Carters Green. Following a resumé of the circumstantial evidence and the Harvey women's account of Lowe's bloodstained clothing, leading to his arrest, Chief Superintendent Whitehurst applied for the prisoner to be remanded in

*James Clark, West Bromwich borough coroner, 1900. (Author's collection)*

5

custody until the next Thursday. In reply to the court clerk's usual question as to whether he had anything to say why he should not be remanded, Lowe answered, 'Only that I was not down that way.'

On the afternoon of Sunday 2 December, the funeral cortège of little Matilda made its way through the silent streets of West Bromwich to the Borough Cemetery at Heath Lane, a journey of about one mile. The chief mourners consisting of her parents, two sisters and grandmother were followed by the pupils and the whole of the teaching staff from St James Day School, Hill Top, which she had formerly attended. It was reported in the press that 'considerably over 10,000 persons' lined the route and every available vantage point within the cemetery. The service was conducted by the Revd J.W. Jones, vicar of St James's Church, in the cemetery chapel where the schoolchildren sang a selection of hymns. The vicar stated that there was a 'profound sympathy amongst the people of the district for the parents in their bereavement under such painful circumstances, and also a feeling of profound horror that such a disgraceful crime had been committed in their midst.' Afterwards, the cortège move to a plot in the cemetery where the unfortunate child was laid to rest in an unmarked grave.

When Lowe made his second appearance at West Bromwich Law Court on Thursday 6 December, it was clear that the great public interest incited by the case continued unabated. Arriving from Birmingham's Winson Green Prison, as he stepped from the prison van, the waiting crowd surged forward, such was the desire manifested by those assembled to catch a glimpse of the accused as he was led to the court cells. Inside the packed courtroom, the proceedings were presided over by Chief Magistrate Councillor John Henry Chesshire JP who held the distinction of being the current serving mayor for the borough of West Bromwich that year. Supporting him were Messrs F.T. Jefferson JP, Heywood Hartland JP, Henry Sutcliffe JP and C. Beech JP. Lowe ascended the stairs leading from the cells and took his place in the dock.

Throughout the proceedings, which only lasted a few minutes, he appeared to treat the matter with the utmost indifference, having both his hands in his trouser pockets and showing no sign of emotion or even the

*Presiding Magistrate, Councillor John Henry Chesshire, JP, serving Mayor of West Bromwich, December 1900. (Author's collection)*

*Henry Sutcliffe, JP. (Author's collection)*

slightest interest whatsoever in the case against him. This was in stark contrast to the previous Tuesday when his brother paid him a visit whilst on remand at Winson Green. Then, it was stated, he 'broke down entirely' following a touching interview, and showed great anxiety about the welfare of his young boy, giving his brother special instructions as to his care. Mr J.S. Sharpe, from local solicitors Sharpe & Darby, was engaged to appear for the accused. Mr Sharpe made no objection when it was decided to remand Lowe for a further week, by which time, it was hoped the earlier adjourned inquest would be concluded. The mayor then addressed the accused, informing him that he would be remanded in custody until the following Thursday. At this, the prisoner picked up his cap, which he had laid down in the dock, and turned to be led back to the cells. He walked away in a cool manner, casting a cursory glance at the spectators seated in the gallery. Outside, as the prison van left the precincts of the law courts for its return journey to Birmingham, the assembled crowd hooted and otherwise demonstrated their indignation against the prisoner. On both journeys to and from courts, Lowe was very quiet in his demeanour and hardly spoke to the prison officers who escorted him. At no time did he make the slightest reference to the terrible crime of which he was accused.

The inquest into the tragedy was resumed at the same law courts by the coroner, Mr James Clark, on the morning of Wednesday 12 December, in the presence of a jury whose foreman was one Mr A.C. Curtler. This time, Mr Clark had the assistance of Mr Harold Arthur Pearson MA, the coroner for South East Staffordshire. Also present were Mr B. Weekes of Birmingham, representing the Treasury who sat in opposition to Mr J.S. Sharpe, defending solicitor, who was accompanied by the prisoner himself.

During the inquiry, which lasted a lengthy seven hours, Louisa Coleyshaw informed Mr Weekes that she only knew the accused from occasionally seeing him pass through the square and was not aware that her daughter knew of him, or to her knowledge that they had ever spoken together. Lowe's mother-in-law, Mary-Ann Harvey, sold lemonade, lettuces and radishes from No. 67 Witton Lane, and Matilda was sometimes sent there to purchase these items. She only ever went in the daytime and the last occasion had been about two months ago.

*Harold Arthur Pearson, MA, coroner for South East Staffordshire, 1900. (Author's collection)*

Attention was then given to the last reported sightings of the girl. Hannah Maria Powell of No. 14 Rydding Square, stated that just before closing time, late in the evening of Monday 26 November, she had fetched some 'supper beer' from the Cottage Spring public house, (then situated at the top of Crookhay Lane, and now rebuilt a little further down) and was returning home along Witton Lane at about 11.05 p.m. When she reached the entrance to Rydding Square, she saw Matilda by the Golden Lion Inn, which stood on the corner of the square with Witton Lane. It was raining heavily, and the child wore a woollen wrap over her head. They didn't speak, but she observed that the girl was walking in the direction of the Junction Inn.

William Davies, a miner from No. 2a Sandpit Cottages, Hateley Heath, was walking home along Witton Lane in the company of a friend named Danks when, as well as observing the soldier Boffey, dressed in Royal Artillery uniform and conversing with three others outside the Cottage Spring around 11.10 p.m., he also saw Matilda (whose name he didn't know, but had seen often before when walking the lane) peering into Harriet Price's shop window at No. 31a Witton Lane, which stood a little way up from the Golden Lion.

The last positive sighting was made by David Hadley, a twelve-year-old schoolboy residing at No. 39 Hateley Heath and well known to the girl. A little earlier, he had assisted to his home a blind man by the name of John Hill, who lived in Holloway Bank, and at 11.15 p.m. was making his way back to Hateley Heath along Witton Lane. When he encountered Matilda, she had by now crossed over the lane and was standing on the stone kerb of the gutter in between the Cottage Spring and Junction Inn. From here led the footpath over the Hilly-Piece to Holloway Bank. Hurrying home in the pouring rain, the boy did not stop for conversation and carried on past. By now the lane appeared to be otherwise deserted.

Following a resumé of the events, concerning the discovery of the body and the later arrest of the accused, the coroner began his summing up, confining his address to only the questions the jurors would be called upon to answer. These were: the cause of death, by what means it was brought about, and by whom. He recounted the circumstantial evidence given during the inquiry, and highlighted that the last positive sighting of the girl was 11.15 p.m. He then stated that considering the statement given to the police by the soldier Boffey as to encountering Lowe in Witton Lane at the same time, there was a strong possibility that the paths of both the victim and accused could have crossed shortly afterwards. They also had to bear in mind the elapsed time before Lowe eventually arrived home to his lodgings and to the condition of the clothing worn that night, most critically of all the presence of the suspicious bloodstains. Mr Clark reminded the jury that the case was either one of murder or nothing else. After a short deliberation in private, foreman of the jury, Mr Curtler, returned the verdict of 'Wilful murder against the accused, Joseph Lowe.'

In a seemingly tight schedule, Lowe was back in court the following day, Thursday 13 December, to face committal proceedings. Once again before the mayor, Councillor J.H. Chesshire JP and fellow Justices of the Peace, Messrs E.H. Stringer, C. Beech, James Edward Wilson and James Scattergood, he was formally charged with causing the death of Matilda Coleyshaw. He continued with the same indifference exhibited during his previous appearances, again sitting with his hands in his pockets, showing not the least sign of anxiety throughout as he listened to the evidence against him. On this occasion, the borough medical officer, Dr Herbert Manley, gave evidence of an examination he had made of the prisoner at the request of the police at West Bromwich Central police station on Friday 30 November. There, the prisoner manifested not only a willingness for this to be done, but also expressed a desire that a thorough examination should take place. Dr Manley declared that the result of his examination was entirely negative and he found no marks indicating any violent act upon the part of the prisoner as had been suggested. With time allowing for only a short hearing that afternoon, an adjournment was made for the case to continue the following day.

The proceedings were resumed with the absence of Messrs Stringer and Wilson from the body of JPs, being replaced instead with

*James Scattergood, JP.*
*(Author's collection)*

*James Edward Wilson, JP.*
*(Author's collection)*

Alderman Samuel Pitt, who, previous to Councillor Chesshire, had held office as mayor of West Bromwich. Magistrate, James Scattergood, raised his concerns about an incident which had arisen the previous day when the twelve-year-old boy, David Hadley, was placed in the witness box and shown the white woollen shawl by Sergeant Owen. He was asked to swear that it was the one he'd seen Matilda Coleyshaw wearing on that fateful night. This he did so. Mr Scattergood argued that because the boy had previously sworn that the colour of the shawl was pink, it was a very underhanded way to go about securing a sworn statement in a court of law. He considered it a most improper thing to have placed the shawl in this way, but did not want to disconcert the boy whilst giving his evidence and had waited until now to raise his objections and draw the matter to the attention of his colleagues. He hoped that nothing of the sort would happen again during the hearing of the case, and that witnesses would swear to what they had seen, the articles being produced afterwards in court so not to shape the evidence.

For the prosecution, Mr Weekes said that he was sorry to hear those remarks from a magistrate, with reference as to the misguided actions of Sergeant Owen, but should like to say that he had attended a great many public prosecutions, and felt that instead of reprimanding, he felt that he must really compliment the officers of that division on the able way in which they had prepared the case. He also stated that he had never known a case more intelligently got up than this one and that he had also noticed the extreme fairness with which they had endeavoured to deal with the case throughout. As the day's proceedings came to a close, the prisoner was committed for trial at the next Stafford Assizes, the date set being Saturday 10 March 1901.

During the intervening period, along with the rest of the British Empire, the attention of the residents of Hill Top was switched to the mourning of Queen Victoria, who had passed away at Osbourne House on the Isle of Wight on 22 January 1901. This, in part, may have explained the diminished interest in the case, evident by the fact that when the judge, Mr Justice Phillimore took his seat on the bench at 10.30 a.m. to oversee the trial on 10 March, not a single spectator occupied the public gallery, and at no time during the proceedings was the courtroom

*Alderman Samuel Pitt, JP, former Mayor of West Bromwich. (Author's collection)*

crowded. Prosecuting for the Crown, the Honourable Mr Lyttleton KC, MP, was assisted by Mr Kettle, barrister. Lowe's defence was taken up by Mr C.F. Vachell, alongside Mr Graham Millward. The charge of 'Wilful Murder' was put to Lowe who replied in a firm and loud voice, 'Not guilty.'

Mr Lyttleton, in opening the case, stated that on 27 November last year, at about 9 a.m. in the morning, the body of the deceased child, Matilda Coleyshaw aged nine, was found in a place called Ball's Hill Field (the Hilly-Piece). The body disclosed terrible signs of violence, not that this was the actual cause of death, but violence leading to the conclusion that the child had been horribly murdered. Suffocation was the decided cause of death. The prosecution, it would be shown, were able to trace the path of the child from 11 p.m. on the night of 26 November from her home at No. 35 Rydding Square, to the start of the footpath over the said field, near the junction of Crookhay Lane with Witton Lane, just fifteen minutes later. In due course, three witnesses would be produced, who possibly had made later sightings of the victim walking to her doom, most probably with the accused, in the direction of where the body was subsequently found. He affirmed that all the evidence would place the accused near to the spot from where the girl disappeared and at the same time also. Crucial to the case, he pointed out, was the time unaccounted for between Lowe's alleged conversation with the witness Boffey at 11.15 p.m. and his eventual return home, just a short walk away, at two minutes to midnight.

First to give evidence was the girl's mother, Louisa, who deposed to the reason for sending her daughter out from the safety of the family home, adding that she had never been away from her sight so late in the night before. Following the testimonies of Hannah Maria Powell, William Davies and the boy, David Hadley, whose evidence (as heard at the resumed inquest the previous December) pieced together the girl's short journey up Witton Lane, the three witnesses, to whom Mr Lyttleton had earlier alluded, were introduced to the court to tell their stories.

Mr James Botford, aged thirty-four, of No. 66 Rydding Square, was returning from an evening out at Wednesbury Theatre, accompanied by his wife, Katherine, and neighbour, Emily Fenn, who lived at No. 76 Rydding Square. It was about 11.30 p.m. when they decided to take a shortcut through the Colliery Road from

Holloway Bank and over the Hilly-Piece. As the threesome were approaching some stumps separating the colliery track from the entrance to the Hilly-Piece, two figures emerged in the gloom a little way ahead, walking with their backs to them. They appeared to be a little girl in the company of a mature man, who, before the trio got any closer, turned towards the abandoned Ball's Hill Colliery and disappeared far out of sight. Although the visibility was quite poor, Emily Fenn noticed that the girl was wearing a white wrap over her head. All three agreed that the little girl appeared to be going with the man willingly. The sighting was only yards from where the body was discovered the next morning.

The court's attention was then directed to the whereabouts of the prisoner Lowe that evening. John (Jack) Hawthorne, landlord of the Bird in Hand public house, Queen Street, Hill Top, confirmed that Lowe had left his premises at closing time, 11 p.m., in the company of John Maybury, who lived further along Queen Street at No. 15. Maybury said he wished 'goodnight' to his drinking companion, who he noticed set off in the direction of Castle Street, adding that he had always found Lowe to be a quiet and inoffensive friend.

Edward Ray Boffey of No. 38 Wheeler's Lane, Birmingham, a horse driver serving in the Royal Artillery and stationed at Colchester, told of spending the evening in the company of his elder brother and two others at the Cottage Spring public house, whilst on furlough. When time was called they stood outside talking for about five minutes before parting with one of the group, George Bunce, and then with his brother and one James McNulty, Boffey began to walk up Witton Lane towards his brother's house, No. 29a, where he was staying.

Outside his brother's house, situated at the top end of Witton Lane, not far from the main highway, the three continued a short conversation when Joseph Lowe entered the lane and exchanged a few pleasantries with them. In a few minutes, they shook hands and parted, Lowe then making his way along Witton Lane towards his lodgings. He would have to pass the wooden stiles leading to the Hilly-Piece on his way. James McNulty, when giving his evidence, said that before continuing towards his home, No. 34 New Street, Hill Top, he had heard Lowe tell Boffey that he might not see him again as he was due to work nightshifts. He agreed that the time they all parted was 11.15 p.m.

At some time during the proceedings, a plan of the locality was produced by the West Bromwich Assistant Borough Surveyor, James Stevenson Hendry. He stated that from the Golden Lion Inn to the lodgings of the accused, No. 67 Witton Lane, was a distance of 70yds, and from the same inn to No. 35 Rydding Square, where the deceased lived was 120yds. Price's shop, No. 31a Witton Lane, was 210yds from the wooden stumps in the Colliery Road, when crossing the Hilly-Piece. From the said stumps to the spot where the body lay was about 66yds in direct line. It could be seen there was a footpath across the Hilly-piece, accessed by the side of the Junction Inn, Witton Lane, which terminated at the elbow bend of the Colliery Road. The Hilly-Piece was bounded by a fence alongside the Colliery Road, and the fence was 3ft 6in in height.

The court heard from Mary-Ann Harvey, the prisoner's mother-in-law, that she had retired to bed at about 11.45 p.m. that night. A little before midnight, she heard the front door open and Lowe exchange just a few words with her husband. She also heard him go into the backyard and return to the house a few minutes later.

Following her account of the discovery of Lowe's wet and bloodstained apparel hidden in the tin trunk beside his bed, forensic scientist Dr Alfred Bostock Hill reported his findings upon examination of the confiscated clothing. He found spots of blood on the right jacket sleeve cuff, just on the inside, and on the right wristband of the shirt cuff a corresponding pattern. He could not, however, conclude that the stains found on the waistcoat and handkerchief were blood. Of the stains visible on the trousers, none were detected as blood. The victim's clothing was also put to test, finding bloodstains on the inside back of her chemise and her bodice stained with blood and 'other matter'.

Towards the end of the trial, Mr Vachell addressed the jury in defence of the accused. Speaking for considerably over an hour, he dwelt upon the responsibility which rested upon the jurors, saying that so revolting was the crime that if the prisoner was found guilty, execution must of necessity follow. It seemed to him that the case, although it contained elements of suspicion, had been placed before the jury in an extraordinarily manner. He contended that it would not be safe to convict the accused on such evidence. Upon the evidence, it was impossible that the prisoner could have come into contact with the girl as it was almost certain from what the witnesses had said that at that very time, the prisoner was talking to the soldier Boffey, outside No. 29a Witton Lane. The true murderer, whoever he was, had meanwhile taken this poor little girl to her doom.

The important point to ascertain, he urged, was the exact time the prisoner left the Boffey's. Up to that point, it was impossible he could have seen the child. It was quite probable that he might have gone as far as the clock at the Board School, and that Sergeant Wilson was mistaken in stating that Lowe had meant the Farley clock tower at Carters Green. If this was so, then the prisoner would have had time to walk up to the Board School and back into the company of the Boffey's. Finally, did the jury think that if the prisoner was the murderer, he could get away with so little blood on his clothing?

Mr Justice Phillimore, in summing up, took exactly one hour. He went minutely through the evidence, especially dwelling upon the question of the times submitted and the statements which the prisoner had made. He agreed that there was not much evidence to connect Lowe with the child, and that whoever the murderer was, he must have been an acquaintance of the girl or someone who was able to exercise a potent influence over her. If the prisoner was the murderer, he certainly had acted with great courage and coolness, and a distinct point in his favour was his behaviour all through. It was remarkable that if the prisoner had done the foul deed there should be so little blood found on his clothing. The jury should not convict the prisoner unless they were reasonably satisfied of his guilt. His Lordship then invited the jury to retire to consider their verdict.

*The Farley clock tower, Carter's Green, West Bromwich, c. 1900. (Author's collection)*

Following a deliberation of one hour and ten minutes, the jury returned to the court at 7.30 p.m. When asked to submit their findings, the foreman of the jury declared 'Guilty of wilful murder!' The judge then assumed the black cap and spoke:

Joseph Lowe, the jury, after a careful trial, in which everything has been said for you that could be said by your counsel, have found you guilty of murder. I must say that I agree with the verdict and that I cannot hold out any hope of a reprieve. The crime was a most cruel one. I have only to beg, entreat and beseech you, that you will use the time that the mercy of the law leaves you to make your peace with God and man. Remember this; it is never too late to repent and make your peace with God. It is now my duty to pass upon you the sentence of the law.

His Lordship then duly passed the death sentence upon Joseph Lowe. He was, however, wrong to cast doubt on the issue of clemency. On Monday 6 May 1901, the prisoner's solicitor, Mr J.S. Sharpe, received a communication from the Home Office intimating that, having fully considered the case, the Home Secretary would advise His Majesty, King Edward, to commute the capital sentence to one of penal servitude for life.

# 2

# PITY THE POOR CHILDREN

*Bilston, 1903*

Walking down Bankfield Road today, alongside the huge Morrisons supermarket on the edge of Bilston town centre, it's hard to imagine that just over a century ago barely more than a rough track existed here. It crossed Bilston Brook, by the way of a tiny brick bridge, and further along spanned the Wolverhampton Level of the Birmingham canal, before terminating at Salop Street in nearby Bradley. All around were abandoned coal shafts and pit mounds, typical of the Black Country in those far off days, the whole landscape grim, desolate and isolated. Only a few homes stood in the vicinity. On the Bradley side of the stream stood Brook Terrace, a row of six cottages set back a little distance from the footpath, whilst on the Bilston side, two empty and dilapidated houses almost hid from view a tiny and much older detached property known as Bankfield Cottage.

It was to this lowly brick residence that James Cartwright came to live in December 1902, along with Mrs Mary Ann Pumphrey. She had been separated from her husband William for the past ten years and had since cohabited with James, together with her eldest son Alfred, aged eleven, and their two younger illegitimate children, Jeremiah, aged nine and Mary Ann, aged six. Although somewhat cramped for their needs, they made a comfortable home of their humble dwelling, which stood in the shadow of the gigantic Messrs John Sankey & Sons Ironworks, but with its well cultivated garden, and for the most part obscured from prying eyes by the tall hedgerow, they almost lived the rural idyll only a quarter of a mile from the centre of busy Bilston town.

At the age of thirty-three, James Cartwright was employed as a puddler at Greenway Bros Ironworks in Bradley, to which, no doubt, he walked daily along Bankfield

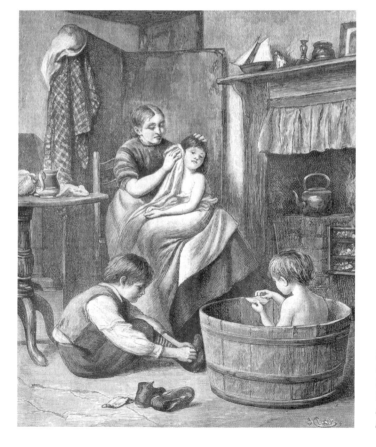

*High Street, Bilston town centre, c. 1903. (Courtesy of Ron Davies)*

*'Although somewhat cramped for their needs, they made a comfortable home of the humble dwelling.' (Author's collection)*

Road. His pastime was keeping poultry, an outhouse at the cottage being given over to several fat geese and ducks. In the garden, he began to construct new fowl pens in furtherance of his hobby. Although he could display a violent temper when under the influence of alcohol, he was otherwise quite a placid man who was very fond of the three children.

On Wednesday 12 August 1903, following a week's absence from work with illness, he visited the surgery of Dr Tomlinson in Bradley, where he was examined by *locum tenens* Dr Nairn, who diagnosed inflammation of the lungs and confined the patient to bed. The following day Dr Nairn visited Bankfield Cottage and found that the condition had worsened to pneumonia. It was decided to bring the patient's bed downstairs to the living room, where he could be better watched over. On the Friday, Dr Nairn was summoned back when Cartwright began to mutter incoherently and point to things that he, but no one else, could see. The doctor found him to be suffering with delirium, a feverish disorder of the mind brought on by his physical condition. His seventeen-year-old niece, Hannah Cartwright, was sent for from his brother Richard's home in Green Lanes, Bilston, to assist with the nursing.

Throughout the day his mentality worsened and he ran about the living room catching unseen things. In the evening though, he seemed much calmer and less irritable, as Mrs Pumphrey saw to tucking the three children into the bed they all shared upstairs at 7.45 p.m.

*Bankfield Road, Bilston. Bankfield Cottage once stood behind the tall bushes. (Author's collection)*

A little after midnight on Saturday 15 August, Mrs Pumphrey herself settled down in the makeshift bed she had set up on the opposite side of the room to where Cartwright lay. Although quiet, he had a peculiar look in his eyes, which caused his companion to doubt his sanity and wonder whether she should remain with him in the same room.

Half an hour later, shortly after she fell into a doze, she was awakened by the creaking of Cartwright's bed as he otherwise silently rose to his feet and stealthily crept across the room to stand and stare over her recumbent figure. Through pierced eyes she saw that he had the look of a madman about him. No doubt he thought the woman was sound asleep. Suspicious of his actions, Mrs Pumphrey sat up alertly, later declaring, 'I thought he was going to murder me there and then.'

Strangely though, Cartwright sunk back into his bed, moaning and groaning in an alarmingly demented fashion. On hearing this, his niece Hannah hurriedly made her way downstairs and entered the room. Terrified, Mrs Pumphrey fetched a glass of milk, which Cartwright drank in a gulp, but was immediately sick. She passed him another glass, then just as she turned around he flew at her demanding she fetch 'a sharp drink'. Trembling from limb to limb, she served him some lemon kali, which no sooner had he consumed, he commenced to attack her.

Mrs Pumphrey fought long and hard as the pair closed in a most fearful battle. His grip was awful, tearing away her garments as she struggled desperately to break free. Finally, his fury spent itself and he began to gasp for breath. Bruised and bloodied, the stricken woman summoned the strength to push her attacker aside and make a run for it, whilst the terrified witness, Hannah, managed to unbolt the door which led into the garden. For a few minutes the two women held the outer door handle tight as Cartwright wrestled with the interior lever intent on pursuit, before withdrawing back into the living room.

Now completely naked, she shouted up to the children to flee the cottage as she ran through the garden and out into the lane closely followed by Hannah. As they crossed the little bridge over the stream and headed towards Brook Terrace, an unearthly chorus of high pitched squeals and shrieks emanated from Bankfield Cottage, piercing the still night air and giving the women to believe that Cartwright was now slaughtering his prized fowl.

Woken by the women's desperate cries for help, half a dozen men and youths set out from Brook Terrace and began to walk towards Bilston town centre to summon police assistance. Passing by Bankfield Cottage they could hear Cartwright smashing the furniture up inside. Meanwhile, the two stricken women sought sanctuary in one of the cottages at Brook Terrace, where Mrs Pumphrey was clothed in whatever apparel could be spared. As they entered the town centre, the posse of neighbours encountered three Bilston lawmen, making their way back to Bradley after locking up an offender they had earlier arrested. On being informed that Cartwright had gone raving mad and had attacked his partner, Police Constables Walley, Robinson and Patrick immediately made for the direction of Bankfield Cottage, accompanied by the concerned inhabitants of Brook Terrace, except for one young man who was sent onwards to Bilston police station to raise the alarm and summon reinforcement officers to the scene.

As the party of locals and lawmen closed in on Cartwright's home, he could be heard still chopping up the furniture and smashing all breakable objects. However, when they entered the garden all the noises abruptly ceased. Now instead, an eerie silence held the investigators in chilled suspense. The door stood ajar and all was in darkness. Police Constable Patrick struck a light and prepared to enter. Suddenly, the door was violently flung shut and the bolt slid across and fastened. All three policemen burst open the door as Cartwright was heard running up the steep and narrow stairs out of sight.

Presently, Mrs Pumphrey heard of the arrival of the police and returned to the scene. She circled the cottage, calling out the names of her children, but could get no response. Now she noticed that the ducks and geese still roosted peacefully in their pens and were quite unharmed. What had made the alarming shrill cries that pierced the night air when she earlier fled the cottage, and why couldn't she get any reply from her three young children? She shuddered as a feeling of intense dread came over her. Maybe, she hoped, the children had slept soundly through all the chaos and commotion of the past hour.

Now the three officers entered the cottage and cautiously approached the bottom of the stairs. Hearing a noise coming from the top of the stairs, Police Constable Patrick called out, 'Is that you Cartwright?'

'No', he shouted back adding, 'You come up here and I shall serve, or do for you, as I have done for the others.' He then threw various missiles down the stairs, directed towards the officers before stepping forward brandishing the broken barrel of an old gun and teasing, 'Come on up.' He refused to descend the stairs threatening, 'I've got something for anyone who comes near me.'

Bravely, Police Constable Patrick, with his baton in one hand, and with the other, shielding his head with the seat of a broken chair, began to climb the stairs. Two steps from the top, Cartwright sprang out from a dark recess and, aiming beneath the makeshift shield, struck the officer a violent blow to the side of the head with the barrel of the gun. The stunned officer reeled backwards, falling down the stairs into the arms of Police Constable Robinson. Cartwright then resumed lobbing a barrage of assorted missiles down the stairs, keeping the officers well at bay.

By now, reinforcements had arrived in the form of Sergeant Carson and Police Constables Day and Findlay. Outside, a ladder was placed against an upstairs window in a failed attempt to distract the madman, who no matter, continued to hold the lawmen off, throwing anything he could lay his hands on, including the gun barrel used to strike Constable Patrick. Sergeant Carson took possession of this weapon and on examining it, found to his horror that it was smeared all over with blood and bits of brain, to which were adhered many fine human hairs. Cartwright had now kept the police at distance for more than an hour. Fears began to be voiced over the welfare of the children, making more urgent the need to apprehend Cartwright and gain access to their sleeping quarters.

A decision was made to storm the stairs. Using the mattress from Cartwright's bed for protection, the officers made a rush up the staircase, forcing their attacker to retreat into the children's bedroom. From inside came the sound of breaking glass, then all fell silent. After a few cautious moments, the officers booted open the bedroom door, and still guarded by the tatty mattress, made a dramatic entrance into the room where the most gruesome and sickening spectacle awaited them.

The ceiling, walls and furniture ran crimson, with blood and brains splashed in all directions. On the blood soaked bed lay the lifeless bodies of all three children, their faces unrecognisable, and their innocent little heads brutally smashed in. The two youngest, Jeremiah and Mary Ann, remained in sleeping position, their battered bodies still tucked in under the bedclothes. Stretched out across them was their partially dressed older brother, Alfred, his legs dangling over the side of the bed, below which, the floor was littered with fragments of shattered skull and also besmeared with yet more congealed blood and brains. The whole apartment bore the appearance and smell of a butcher's slaughterhouse.

In a corner of the room, close to the bed, Cartwright sank to a crouched position and cowered. Blood wept from a self-inflicted wound in his throat, made with a piece of broken window pane. He was calm but appeared to be utterly exhausted. Completely worn out in strength, he was seized and handcuffed by Constables Day and Findlay, offering no resistance to arrest. Too exhausted to walk, it was necessary for the officers to literally drag him out of the room and down the stairs. Whilst leading him outside, Police Constable Patrick asked, 'Well, Jim, what have you done this for?' An insane grin crept over Cartwright's face as he stared intently at the officer and callously replied, 'Only a bit of fun!'

At 3 a.m., Superintendent Spendlove arrived to take charge of the detained man. As dawn broke over the Black Country, he surveyed the scene. Outwardly the only clue to the earlier dramatic events was the shattered bedroom window. In contrast, well tended plants filled the kitchen window below, further enhanced with a pretty display of seasonal flowers in an outside window box. On entering the cottage, the superintendent was met with a picture of systematic destruction. Everywhere, the floors were littered with smashed pieces of furniture, and household utensils lay shattered where they were thrown. Such was the range and volume of missiles thrown down the stairs, that it was miraculous no officer had come to any harm, other than the blow to the head Police Constable Patrick had received from the raging Cartwright.

In the bedroom, his gaze cast over the most unbelievable carnage imaginable, it now being more reminiscent of an abattoir than the cosy sleeping quarters, where Mrs Pumphrey had lovingly bade her three children goodnight. The grim sight of their brutally battered bodies lying slumped together on the blood-soaked bed would surely haunt forever the courageous policemen who bore witness to the horrific spectacle enacted in Bilston that night. Amongst the sickly mush that fouled the floor lay the broken stock of Cartwright's gun, bearing testimony to the excessive force used in carrying out his murderous attacks on the three defenceless innocents.

The monster was conveyed to the town's police station, situated in Mount Pleasant on the corner of the aptly named Bow Street, and there placed in a holding cell, where, owing to his earlier attempted suicide, a constant watch was kept.

Later that morning as shops and inns opened up for business, news of the awful tragedy spread through Bilston town centre. Eyewitnesses to the night's sensational events drew crowds of thrilled news seekers in the town's busy market. Soon, Bankfield Cottage was the cynosure of all eyes, as crowds of morbid sightseers flocked to the unassuming little property, tramping about the garden and peering in through its tiny shattered windows. By midday, thousands had converged on the scene, occupying surrounding pit mounds and any other lofty vantage point to obtain a better view. Many travelled from districts several miles away from Bilston, some taking snapshots, while others busied themselves making impromptu pencil sketches. Collections were made by about a dozen people using cigar boxes, on the lids of which was written, 'Pity the poor children'.

That afternoon, Cartwright was brought before Dr S. Ashley Smith JP in a special court held at Bilston police station, and charged with having wilfully murdered the three unfortunate children. He was described by the press as 'being of medium height, clad in ironworker's attire, and his shirt being thickly besmeared with blood. Around his neck was a bandage, the front of which was also clotted with blood, corresponding with the cut inflicted to the throat. He also bore a gaping wound in the left arm.' Dr Smith explained that before attending court, he had made a thorough medical examination of the prisoner, deciding that he was in a fit enough condition to be moved from his cell and face the charges put to him.

*'Others busied themselves making impromptu pencil sketches.' (Author's collection)*

Superintendent Spendlove gave evidence that, from what Mrs Pumphrey had told him at the scene of the crime, and in the presence of Cartwright, he ascertained that the man had attacked the woman during the night, but following a struggle, she made her escape from the cottage. Between the time of her flight and the arrival of the police officers, the children were evidently murdered in the brutal manner described to the court.

The magistrate asked Cartwright, 'Do you want to ask the superintendent any questions?'

'No, sir.' he replied. When asked if he had any reason why he should not be remanded in custody until the following Friday, he gave the same answer. Cartwright, who appeared to be half stupefied, was then led from the court by Sergeant Gibbs and Police Constable Godwin. Back at the police station, Dr Kendrick attended to stitch up the wound in the prisoner's left arm, before his removal to Stafford Prison.

Meanwhile, at the Great Western Hotel in Hall Street, South Staffordshire coroner, Mr T. Allen Stokes opened the inquest upon the three tragic children. Evidence of identification was given by Hannah Cartwright who, at the tender age of seventeen, had carried out the formidable task at the mortuary earlier in the day. The coroner declared that the identification was the only evidence he could take for the time being, due to the fact no post-mortems had yet been carried out. He therefore adjourned the inquiry, also until the following Friday. Dr Smith was evidently a rather diligent man, for on that Saturday evening, he also carried out the aforesaid post-mortems on the three little bodies at Bilston Mortuary.

The following day, it still being the weekend, thousands more descended on Bankfield Cottage, eager to see for themselves the stage where one of the most dramatic tragedies in the annals of the Black Country had been acted out. The appearance of the grieving mother, accompanied by Sergeant Carson, must have been something of a bonus for the assembled sensation seekers, as she entered the cottage in search of 'something she had left behind', which transpired to be a pawn ticket.

The joint funeral of the three little victims was carried out on the afternoon of Wednesday 19 August. At 2.30 p.m., in the presence of a surging crowd, three tiny coffins were brought out of the mortuary and placed in a hearse to be conveyed to Bankfield Cottage. All along the route, spectators gathered in awed silence to witness the pathetic spectacle. At the cottage, mourners were joined by many hundreds of reverent sightseers, some perched on walls or gates and any other conceivable vantage point they could occupy.

As the cortège formed, it could be seen that several choice wreaths contributed by family and friends had been laid upon the coffins. Mrs Pumphrey wept bitterly as she led the cortège the short distance to St Luke's Church in nearby Market Street, where the Revd W. Prosser performed the first half of the proceedings. Afterwards, four girls attired in white and carrying posies of flowers, and also four boys, likewise carrying posies and wearing white gloves, headed the procession to Bilston Cemetery. Now the father of the eldest victim, a night manager at Bilston Steelworks, joined the cortège on the solemn journey.

*Stafford Prison, c. 1903. (Author's collection)*

The whole route was lined with huge crowds of spectators, evoked into a remarkable demonstration of mass sympathy. From the cemetery gates to the graveside, the coffins where borne by fellow pupils of the school that the children had attended. During the internment, the Revd Prosser, again officiating, addressed the assembled multitude with much emotion saying, 'I dare not trust myself to speak concerning this event today, but will do so on Sunday evening in the church.' Afterwards, the mourners, many with tearful eyes, quietly melted away.

A court hearing due to be held on Friday 21 August had to be cancelled, on receiving news from Stafford Prison that Cartwright was too unwell to leave the prison infirmary. Also, the inquest which was to have resumed the same day had to be postponed because of the unavailability of the post-mortem results.

On Friday 28 August, at the Great Western Hotel, the South Staffordshire coroner, Mr T. Allen Stokes, finally resumed the inquest into the deaths of the Pumphrey children, beginning at 1 p.m. in the afternoon. Dr S. Ashley Smith was called to submit his post-mortem examination results and dutifully obliged. He stated that Alfred, the eldest child aged eleven, had the right side of his face smashed in and also suffered a broken jaw. Bruising to his right hand and arm was consistent with supposed attempts to fend off the blows. Jeremiah, aged nine, was killed by a massive fracture to the skull measuring 8in long. Little Mary Ann, aged only six years, was also frightfully battered about the head, the whole of her facial bones being broken.

Listening to the harrowing evidence in stunned silence were the gentlemen of the coroner's jury, comprising the foreman, Mr W. Delaney, and also Messrs George Tubb, Samuel Turner, William Slater, William Shale, John Lester, Louis McCourt, Alfred Edwards, Jesse Thomas, Edward Jones, William Millard Whitehouse, George Lawrence and William Darby.

Mrs Mary Ann Pumphrey, giving evidence, said that for the past ten years, she had been separated from her husband, William, he being the natural father of her eldest child. The younger two were the illegitimate offspring of James Cartwright, with whom she had co-habited at various addresses in the locality for all of that time. About eight months earlier, they had taken possession of Bankfield Cottage.

On Thursday 13 August, she was obliged to remove his bed downstairs to nurse him through a bout of pneumonia. In the small hours of Saturday the 15th, he savagely assaulted her and she fled the property in a naked state, seeking refuge with neighbours at nearby Brook Terrace, leaving behind the three children, all asleep in the one bed upstairs. The concerned neighbours summoned the assistance of the police and on their arrival, she returned to the scene, calling out to her children, but gaining no reply. In between her pitiful sobs, the poor woman told the jury 'I did not think that he would kill them.'

At the request of the coroner, the two halves of the alleged murder weapon were produced. The gun, she explained, was kept hanging from a wooden beam in the living room, but could not be fired. Cartwright only kept it because it had been a favourite of his father's.

Police Sergeant Carson told of recovering the heavily bloodstained barrel from the kitchen floor, after it had been used to strike Constable Patrick on the head, then thrown downstairs as an improvised missile. The broken stock was later found on the bedroom floor, having separated from its counterpart during the frenzied attack on the defenceless children. Following a short retirement, the foreman, Mr Delaney, announced that the jury had reached a verdict of 'Wilful murder in all three deaths against James Cartwright.'

Friday 4 December 1903 saw the commencement of Staffordshire Winter Assizes. Before opening the court, the judge, Mr Justice Bighain, paraded to church, accompanied by the High Sheriff; Mr Charles Tertius Mander MA, JP, the High Sheriff's chaplain; the Revd Alfred Penny MA, Rector of Wolverhampton and Mr S.G. Lovatt, the Mayor of Stafford. The Grand Jury, on being sworn in, read like a Staffordshire *Who's Who*, including; Sir Charles Michael Wolseley, Baronet, of Wolseley Hall, and Mr Henry Vaughan JP, president of Wolverhampton Chamber of Commerce.

The trial of James Cartwright was heard on the second day of the proceedings, Saturday 5 December. Prosecuting was Mr C.F. Vachell, assisted by Mr H. Staveley Hill, whilst the defence was fought by Mr R.J. Lawrence. When called upon to plead, Cartwright declared, 'I know nothing about it at all.'

Mr Vachell told the jury that the case was not a difficult one to prove. The important point for them to consider was the condition of the prisoner's mind

*Sir Charles Michael Wolseley, Bart and Henry Vaughan, JP. Two Grand Jurors from James Cartwright's trial. (Author's collection)*

when he committed the brutal acts. He then explained the known facts of the events, stating:

> For a number of years, the prisoner has worked at Greenway Bros Ironworks at Bradley, and for the last ten years, he has lived with a woman named Pumphrey, who had a child by her own husband and also two other illegitimate children by Cartwright. It is these three children whom the prisoner is charged with murdering. On 12 August this year, the prisoner felt unwell and visited a doctor, who came to the conclusion that his patient was suffering from inflammation of the lungs. The doctor visited the prisoner at his home the following day and found his condition to be rather more serious. When he visited again the next day, he ascertained that the prisoner had been suffering from delirium, arising from the inflammation.

He continued:

> Mrs Pumphrey made arrangements for watching the prisoner during the night of 14 August. The three children were put to bed upstairs, and Mrs Pumphrey decided to sleep in the living room, downstairs, with the prisoner, calling in his niece to assist her. During the night, the prisoner became very restless, and Mrs Pumphrey got up and gave him a draught of milk, but it did not agree with him. He became very violent and no doubt he was in a state of delirium. He attacked Mrs Pumphrey, tore her clothes away and struck her, and she, together with his niece, escaped from the cottage and took refuge in the house of a neighbour. The police were sent for, and very shortly, Constable

Patrick entered the cottage. Hearing a noise up the stairs, he called out 'Is that you, Cartwright?' to which came the reply 'You come up here and I shall do for you as I have done for the others.' Constable Patrick bravely ascended the stairs, but in cautiously looking around when at the top of the stairs to see where he was, the prisoner struck him on the head with a gun barrel. This, amongst other missiles, was then thrown down the stairs at the policemen to prevent them from detaining the prisoner. Other officers arrived and they succeeded in getting upstairs, where they found the prisoner, calm but exhausted, cowering in the children's bedroom.

The jury listened in appalled silence as Mr Vachell described the discovery of the wicked crime, saying:

The police found that the three children were dead, and that their heads had been battered in, blood and brain being scattered about the room. When the broken gun was examined, it was found to be smeared with the same. The prisoner had attempted to end his life by cutting his throat, but in the prison infirmary made a good recovery.

In Cartwright's defence, Mr Lawrence said:

During the time he has been in gaol, the prisoner has been under the observation of Dr Dyer, the prison medical officer, who was of the opinion that at the time the acts were committed, the prisoner, from the state of his health, suffering as he was from delirium, was not responsible for his actions.

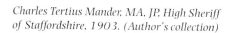

He called on Mrs Pumphrey to take the witness stand, and enquired upon the prisoner's conduct prior to his illness and the subsequent incident. She answered that they had lived very happily together, adding that Cartwright had been very fond of the children.

By direction of the judge, Dr Nairn, assistant to Dr Tomlinson, was called at this stage, and stated that when the prisoner called to see him, he found that he was suffering from inflammation of the lungs, and that his temperature was 103 degrees Fahrenheit. Mr Vachell inquired, 'What is the normal?' '98.4' replied Dr Nairn

*Charles Tertius Mander, MA, JP, High Sheriff of Staffordshire, 1903. (Author's collection)*

*The Revd Alfred Penny, MA, the High Sheriff's Chaplain, 1903. (Author's collection)*

The judge remarked, 'That was a very high temperature for a man to be walking about, was it not?'

The doctor agreed, saying, 'Yes, it was very dangerous. I ordered the patient home, and on visiting the following day found him to be suffering from delirium.'

'Is a person suffering from inflammation of the lungs liable to delirium?' asked the judge.

'Yes,' answered Dr Nairn.

'And sometimes has to be held down?' continued the judge.

'Yes,' confirmed Dr Nairn.

Dr Dyer, the medical officer for Stafford Prison was the last witness to be called. He explained that he had kept the prisoner under close observation in gaol since his committal. The prisoner was rather excited for the first few nights, but he had since been quite rational. He thought that at the time the offences were committed, the prisoner was suffering from delirium, owing to inflammation of the lungs, otherwise pneumonia, and did not know what he was doing.

In his summing up of the case, Mr Justice Bighain told the jury, 'The question you have to answer is whether you think the prisoner, when he murdered the children, did or did not know what he was doing.' The jurors returned a verdict of 'guilty', but adding that at the time of the crimes being committed, the prisoner was not responsible for his actions. His Lordship then ordered that the prisoner should be detained during His Majesty's pleasure.

# 3

# A CHINESE PUZZLE

Just beyond industrial Smethwick, where Matthew Boulton famously developed the steam engine in partnership with James Watt, and also where giant lenses were produced for the world's lighthouses at Chance Brothers Glassworks, lie Warley Woods. It is a green and rustic oasis of 100 acres, close to where Birmingham meets with the Black Country, and once under the jurisdiction of the former Oldbury Urban District Council. The woods form part of an historic parkland laid out in about 1795 by Humphrey Repton, where the impressive Gothic Revival mansion of Warley Abbey was built for Hubert Barclay Galton in 1820, but sadly demolished in 1957.

Warley Woods were saved from residential development during a campaign spearheaded by Alexander M. Chance JP, culminating with their official opening as a public park in June 1906, celebrated with much civic rejoicing. Thirteen years later to the month, celebrations of another kind, those marking the close of the First World War, were marred by one of the most brutal murders to have ever been enacted within our shores.

Late in the afternoon of Friday 27 June 1919, a local schoolboy, Herbert Wilson of Bearwood Road, wandered into a fenced-off spinney, where in this secluded spot he made a horrific discovery. Forty yards from the path and well hidden in a hollow, he stumbled upon a man's brutally battered body, lying on his back in a huddled up position. A worn trilby hat covered the face and a heavily bloodstained towel was wrapped around the victim's neck. Also across the neck lay a heavy wooden log, which appeared to have once belonged to a nearby rustic bench. The shocked youth made a hasty departure from Warley Woods, summoning Police Inspector Francis Drew, who arrived at the crime scene by 5.15 p.m.

Removal of the trilby revealed the victim to be a Chinaman, 5ft 6in in height, and endowed with a splendid muscular physique. The body was conveyed to Oldbury

*Gothic Warley Abbey, which was demolished in 1957. (Author's collection)*

Mortuary, where Dr Louis Charles Broughton, from Langley House, carried out a post-mortem examination. The injuries he found were varied and considerable in extent.

A large contused wound on the forehead looked as though it may have been inflicted with a hammer. The lower jaw was fractured in three places, along with the breast bone and three ribs. These injuries were probably made with the log of wood, which weighed 41lbs, being used as a battering ram. There were at least twenty-four stab wounds to the cartilage of the left ear, and a deep puncture wound behind the same ear which led down to a fracture at the base of the skull. Near to the right ear were four cuts, one of them identical to the deep puncture wound behind the left ear, which also led down to a similar fracture also at the base of the skull. These wounds must have been caused by a succession of blows delivered with great violence. The weapon used must have been a long sharp chisel or some such instrument. In addition, there were six lacerated wounds to one side of the head and four to the other, but more sinister were the many ghastly and bizarre mutilations made to the chest, probably while the victim was still alive. The doctor concluded that death had taken place at least forty-eight hours prior to the discovery of the body and that the victim had been 'Foully and most brutally murdered.'

The police found themselves with an intriguing puzzle on their hands. Who was the mysterious Chinaman? Why had he met with an extremely violent death in Warley

*The entrance to Warley Woods. (Author's collection)*

Woods and by whom? The first part of the puzzle was solved on Monday 30 June when Li Ding Ting, a Chinaman lodging at an address in Coleshill Street, Birmingham, reported as missing Zee Ming Wu, a compatriot and one of five fellow lodgers. Ting identified the corpse as that of his friend, explaining that he had last seen him alive when he had left for work at Wright's Eagle Range factory in Thimblemill Lane, Smethwick, on Monday 23 June. Inquiries revealed that Wu had finished work at 5.15 p.m. but failed to turn up at the factory the following day and had not been seen since.

Zee Ming Wu was aged forty-three and a native of Shanghai, where it was believed he had a wife and family. Described as a quiet, respectable and rather reticent man, he had few associates. He busied himself with building up his post office savings account, which stood at £240, and harboured desires to earn enough money to return to China and settle back with his kinsfolk. A search of his lodgings revealed that his savings account book was missing, although £5 in loose change was found amongst his possessions and 1s ½d had been discovered in his clothing at the crime scene.

An inquest was held at Oldbury Public Buildings on Tuesday 1 July conducted by Mr A.H. Hebbert, who stated that 'No good purpose could be served by adjourning the inquiry.' He added 'There could be no question that the man had been foully and brutally murdered and the police would continue their investigations.' A witness, Mr George William Jones, had come forward, declaring that at 7.45 p.m. on Monday 23 June, four days previous to the discovery of the body, he had seen two Chinamen entering Warley Woods, and on being shown a photograph of Zee Ming Wu, agreed that he was one of the two aforementioned men.

*Freeth Street, Oldbury. The Public Buildings are on the left of the picture. (Author's collection)*

This information encouraged the police to concentrate their enquiries amongst the Chinese community in Birmingham. Working together, Oldbury police and Birmingham Criminal Investigation Department soon made an arrest. Inspector Drew, accompanied by Inspector Barnes of the CID, visited a house in Bristol Street, Birmingham, and for an undisclosed reason, arrested a thirty-year-old Chinaman, Ah Chee, on suspicion of having caused the death of Zee Ming Wu. Chee, who travelled daily to work at the Malcast Foundry in Walsall was, like the victim, a native of Shanghai. Placed in an identity parade along with seven other Chinamen and two others of English origin on Wednesday 9 July, he was picked out by George William Jones as the man seen entering Warley Woods with the victim on the evening of Monday 23 June.

Tall and smartly dressed in a brand new dark grey suit, but wearing no collar or tie, he made an appearance before Mr W.S. Rollason JP at a special court held in Oldbury the following day. An interpreter named So Fan was engaged to translate for the defendant, who, when charged with the murder replied, 'If murder, did anyone see me do it? I did not do this. I did not know that Zee Ming Wu was murdered until three days afterwards.' Through the interpreter, he was asked if he had any questions to put to the court. He replied 'If anybody saw me do it, what day was it and what time?' For the police, Superintendent Milsom from Oldbury asked for a remand in custody until the following Tuesday. When asked if he had anything to say why he should not be remanded in custody, he said, 'I never did it, so what is the use of keeping me here? When you find out the truth, what are you going to do for me? I am losing wages.' At his second court appearance, the police could offer no evidence against him and so Ah Chee was discharged by the magistrates. Three other Chinamen questioned had earlier been released.

For the next six weeks inquiries drew a blank. During the previous twelve months, there had been four other murders amongst the British Chinese community and not one perpetrator had yet been brought to justice. Just as it began to appear that the slaughter of Zee Ming Wu would also remain unsolved, a sensational and very unexpected line of enquiry developed. Oldbury police received a thrilling communication from the London police force that saw investigating officers boarding the next available train to the capital, in anticipation of some conclusive answers to the Warley Woods puzzle.

It transpired that during the afternoon of Tuesday 24 June, the day after Zee Ming Wu was last seen alive, a Chinaman entered a branch of the post office in Blyth Road, West Kensington Gardens. He presented to the counter clerk, Mr P. Marr, a post office savings book credited with £240 and requested to withdraw the whole amount. When given a withdrawal form to complete, the clerk noticed that he had unsuccessfully tried to copy the signature that appeared on the savings book and became suspicious. Mr Marr invited the Chinaman to accompany him to the head office where he would be asked to produce his passport, but on the way, he became nervous saying, 'Me no go.' He tried to snatch the savings book from the clerk's hand but Mr Marr held it firmly. He decided to return to Blyth Road, when, on arrival, the Chinaman stated, 'Me hungry. Me want my dinner.' Mr Marr asked, 'Will you come back?' The Chinaman guilefully replied, 'Yes.' Of course, he never returned.

Almost exactly a month later, in the early hours of Friday 25 July, police were summoned to investigate the brutal assault and robbery of a Chinaman named Kuo Doung Dsou at No. 15 Aldine Street, Shepherd's Bush. Whilst in bed, he had been beaten about the head with a hammer wielded by a compatriot, Djang Djin Sung, who periodically lodged with the victim when visiting London. Leaving the unconscious man for dead, the fiend fled the scene with £7 in stolen cash, dumping the bloodstained weapon during his escape.

Three weeks later, following an intensive manhunt, Djang Djin Sung was picked up and brought in for questioning. The thirty-three-year-old gave his address as No. 73 Balsall Heath Road, Birmingham, another boarding house at the disposal of Chinese nationals. Whilst in custody, he was identified as the Chinaman who had attempted to use the stolen savings account book at Blyth Road post office two months previously. Oldbury police had already been contacted about this matter, for the savings book was addressed to No. 109 Coleshill Street, Birmingham, and bore the signature of Warley Woods murder victim Zee Ming Wu!

While Kuo Doung Dsou recovered in hospital, a police search of his home in Aldine Street produced some letters and postcards written by Sung referring to the Warley Woods murder. In one of them he wrote 'Zee Ming Wu is buried. He has had no revenge yet. I think the police are careless.' On 11 July, he wrote a letter which stated:

After all, the real offender has been caught. I am not the one. One could not murder Zee Ming Wu for nothing, and if the savings book was taken to London, that must have been the object. Both yesterday and today, the offender has been summoned to court and he has been remanded. Today I see in the newspaper that there were four Chinamen concerned in the murder.

His allusion to the 'real offender' was a reference to the arrest of Ah Chee, who was later discharged from the court. The hammer was also recovered and proved to be the one that Sung used in his workplace at Birmingham.

Whilst under police questioning about the brutal assault on Kuo Doung Dsou, Sung admitted his complicity in the Warley Woods murder, a charge which he faced when making his second court appearance in West London on Saturday 6 September. He had earlier been remanded in custody, charged with the attempted murder of Kuo Doung Dsou. Sung stood between two prison warders as Mr Travers Humphreys, prosecuting for the Crown, told the court that the hammer used in the attack on Dsou was traced back to Sung without 'any shadow of doubt' and must also have been the weapon used to inflict the wounds to Zee Ming Wu in the attack at Warley Woods. He also revealed that two post office staff had identified Sung as the man who tried to obtain £240 by deception at Blyth Road on 24 June.

Sensational statements were read out in which Sung dramatically implicated one Li Ting Jig in the crime, he being a fellow lodger with Wu at Coleshill Street. One statement read:

> I went to work in Birmingham on 23 June. When I left at 5.30 p.m., four Chinamen, including Li Ting Jig and Zee Ming Wu met me. Jig asked me to steal a hammer. I gave the hammer to Jig. We all took the hammer to Warley Woods and we went to the lonely spot. It was about 7 p.m. Jig told me that Wu's parents had cheated his family out of money at the police court in China and said he was going to kill him. Jig said to Wu 'Look, there's a rabbit.' Wu looked around and Jig hit him on the head with the hammer. He gave him one, two, or three taps with the hammer. I took the savings book from the lining of his jacket. Jig told me he kept it there. I carried the dead man to a tree. I picked up the hammer and came away with Jig. He told me to go to London the next day and get the money.

Another read:

> Me take book to post office, but no tell Wu. The book was given me by Jig, who is a very clever businessman. He said, 'You go to London and get the money, and me wait here.'

Mr Humphreys told the court that far from Li Ting Jig being the murderer in this awful case, he would actually be called as a witness for the prosecution at Sung's trial.

On Saturday 13 September, Sung made his third appearance at West London Police Court. Whilst Mr Humphreys was in discussion with Dr Broughton about the probable causes of the victim's injuries, a long chisel-like instrument was produced.

Above: *Inside Warley Woods, c. 1919.* (*Author's collection*)

Left: *Warley Woods today.* (*Author's collection*)

Described to the court as a 'graying' tool, it was said to be similar to instruments used in Sung's workplace. Dr Broughton said 'If I wished to produce such wounds behind the ears, that is just the weapon I should use.'

At this point, the prisoner sprang from his seat in the dock and interrupted with many remarks and gestures, evidently intended as a denial. Mr Humphreys turned to Sung and said, 'No, no, that is not the actual weapon, but is said to be the kind of instrument the murderer used.' Sung continued to gesticulate in an attempt to make himself understood, when his counsel observed: 'He is trying to show how the tool is used in the ordinary way.' Sung nodded in agreement and returned to his seat. The prisoner interrupted again when Li Ting Jig, in giving evidence, stated that he last saw Zee Ming Wu alive on Sunday afternoon, 22 June. Sung again left his seat and cried out, 'No, no, it is all lies. It is between him and me.'

Mr Arthur Grosvenor, at whose house Sung lodged, told the court that the accused had lived at his address in Balsall Heath Road from May 1919 until the middle of July. On the supposed day of the murder, 23 June, Sung returned home late at night, sometime after 11 p.m. After the discovery of the body on 27 June, Sung ran downstairs in the night and told Mr Grosvenor that he was nervous and could not sleep. He said there were a lot of wicked people around and he was afraid to sleep alone in his room because of the murder at Warley Woods. Sung asked if he could sleep in his landlord's room, which he did on the nights of the 27, 28 and 29 June.

Later, he asked Mr Grosvenor the best route to Warley Woods and said that he wanted to go there. He told of visiting the mortuary to view the body and described to his landlord how it had been badly knocked about and mutilated. Mr Grosvenor asked him if he had any suggestions as to who had committed the murder and he replied 'An Englishman.' Mr Grosvenor remarked that an Englishman would not be so brutal. Sung then suggested that it must have been an Italian.

The trial of Djang Djin Sung was held before Mr Justice Rowlatt at Worcester Assizes on Wednesday 22 October 1919. Mr Powell KC, assisted by Mr A.E.N. Jordan, outlined the case for the prosecution, stating that:

> Zee Ming Wu was a respectable and diligent man who had put by £240 in a post office savings account. He went to work on Monday 23 June and stayed at his employment until 5.15 p.m. From that time, nothing is clear of his whereabouts, except that his horrifically mutilated body was found by schoolboy Herbert Wilson in Warley Woods on Friday 27 June.
>
> On Tuesday 24 June, Djang Djin Sung entered Blyth Road post office in West Kensington Gardens, London, and produced the savings book of the dead man in an attempt to unlawfully obtain £240 cash. The desk clerk noticed that Sung had forged the victim's signature and when challenged, he made good his escape.

Mr Reginald Coventry, counsel for the defence, told how Sung had said, 'Me take book to London. Me no kill Wu. The book was given me by Li Ting Jig, who is a very clever businessman.' He alleged Jig had said 'You go to London, me wait here.'

Evidence was given by Li Ting Jig who told the court that he was a fellow lodger with Zee Ming Wu at No. 109 Coleshill Street, Birmingham. He said:

> I have known Zee Ming Wu for some time, but not from China. Sung visited the lodging house in Coleshill Street and spoke with the deceased about money. Sung owed 30s and had called to pay it back, but Zee Ming Wu refused it, telling his visitor that he had £5 in his pocket.

He told how his friend last spoke to him on the afternoon of Sunday 22 June. That was the last time he saw him alive. Zee Ming Wu failed to return to the lodging house after work the following day. Li Ting Jig said that he returned home himself at 6.15 p.m. and did not go out again that night, retiring to bed at 9.30 p.m. Mr Coventry asked the witness 'You knew Wu had a lot of money?'

'Yes', came the reply.

'And that he had it in the post office savings account?' continued the barrister, to which Li Ting Jig answered 'Yes.' Asked if he heard a suggestion that four Chinamen were involved in the murder, he confirmed that his landlady had told him so.

Mr Coventry put it to him: 'Did you tell the accused that Wu's father had cheated your brother out of a lot of money in China?'

'No', answered the witness. 'There was no trouble between our two families in China.'

'I suggest to you that you went to Warley Woods with the accused and Wu, and that once there, you pointed out a rabbit to distract the victim.' ventured the barrister. This was denied by the witness, as was also the suggestion that he had hit Wu on the head with the hammer, and then given his savings account book to Sung, with instructions to withdraw its contents in London. When Li Ting Jig was excused from the witness box, Sung sprang to his feet and protested 'He murder, he murder, no me, no me.'

The prisoner was put in the witness box and told the court that when under police questioning he couldn't properly understand what was being asked, so always answered with 'Yes.' He denied that he murdered Zee Ming Wu. 'Who did commit the murder?', asked Mr Coventry.

'Li Ting Jig', he replied.

'What with?', enquired his defence.

'By the chopper', answered Sung.

In cross-examination of the prisoner, Mr Powell asked for the hammer that was recovered from the London crime scene to be produced. He prompted Sung to tell the court about how it came into his possession. He explained that it was used in his workplace and that Li Ting Jig asked him to steal it from there. He insisted that he didn't know what it would be used for. 'Was Wu killed with that hammer?' asked Mr Powell. 'Yes,' answered Sung.

'Were you standing nearby?'

'Yes', he answered again. The grilling continued:

*Mr Powell:* 'Did you know that he was going to be killed?'

*Sung:* 'I didn't know.'

*Mr Powell:* 'Did you help to carry the body away once Wu had been killed?'

*Sung:* 'Yes.'

*Mr Powell:* 'Did you take the savings book from his coat?'

*Sung:* 'Yes.'

*Mr Powell:* 'Did you take the savings book to London and attempt to collect £240?'

*Sung:* 'Yes.'

*Mr Powell:* 'Did you take the hammer to London, and there dispose of it?'

*Sung:* 'Yes.'

In his summing up, Mr Justice Rowlatt declared that it was extraordinarily difficult not to feel that the words of the accused were a confession. He said, 'Supposing his evidence to be true, it was incredible that he should have rushed down to London with the savings book and the hammer. Such conduct hardly pointed to him being an unwilling and surprised party to the matter'.

The jury took only nine minutes to return their verdict, the foreman declaring the prisoner to be, 'guilty as charged'. His Lordship then duly assumed the black cap and passed the sentence of death upon Sung. Appeal would now be his only hope of a reprieve. The hearing for this was held at Worcester Court of Criminal Appeal on Monday 17 November, presided over by the Lord Chief Justice. Mr Reginald Coventry continued his role in defending the condemned man.

In application of the appeal, Mr Coventry said:

> The murder victim was another Chinaman named Zee Ming Wu, whose body was found on 27 June in Warley Woods. The manner in which Wu met his death was important to the appeal. No doubt he had been stunned by a severe blow to the forehead, probably with some instrument like a hammer, but the doctors said that blow alone did not kill him. Death resulted from two wounds, one on each side of the head, which had been inflicted by some long pointed instrument. The man had been cut about the ears and there were other acts of mutilation. The death was a mystery for something like a month. Sung was arrested and charged with some other offence before being connected with the deceased man's post office savings book. He then made a statement which implicated him in the murder. Apart from that statement the evidence against him was negligible. Apart from that statement there were no facts upon which they could possibly find that this man was guilty of murder.

The Lord Chief Justice interrupted, 'You must not take it that we assent to that proposition'. Mr Coventry continued:

> The statement made by my client was to the effect that another Chinaman, named Li Ting Jig, committed the murder whilst he was present, but that he took no part in

the crime. On Sunday 22 June, Sung went to Wu's lodgings in Birmingham, where five other Chinamen also lived, with the intention of returning 30s he had borrowed from him. Wu said that he did not want the money back as he had £5 in his pocket. There was no suggestion at the time that they were on anything but good terms with each other. Wu, after leaving work the following day, was never seen again until his mutilated body was found in Warley Woods. Sung didn't return home that Monday night until 11 p.m.

The Lord Chief Justice pointed out, 'His own statement is that he was present at the murder'.

'That does not make him guilty of that crime', responded Mr Coventry.

'Is there evidence he knew when he went there, the man who, according to him committed the murder, intended to commit it?' asked his Lordship.

'There is nothing except a single sentence in his statement to the police upon which you could hang that peg', replied the barrister.

Mr Coventry continued:

On the Tuesday Sung travelled to London with the stolen savings account book and attempted to forge Wu's signature to claim £240 from the post office. The counter clerk became suspicious and demanded he produce his passport, which made Sung nervous and run away. The learned judge at the trial had described that episode as cogent evidence of murder. That was putting it too high. It was evidence of larceny, and was highly suspicious, but nothing more than that. Sung returned to Birmingham the following day, then on the Friday, being afraid, he asked his landlord to sleep in the same room because, he said, 'There is a Chinaman found dead and a lot of wicked people are around'. On the Sunday he said he wanted to go to Warley Woods and asked his landlord the best way to get there. That did not look like the actions of a guilty man. When he came back he went to the mortuary to see the body of Wu and told his landlord how badly it was mutilated and what a brutal murder it was.

Mr Coventry contended that those facts were hardly consistent with Sung being guilty of the murder. On such evidence he thought the condemned ought not to have been convicted of the murder. He argued that he was asked in court to undertake the defence of a prisoner without the assistance of a solicitor, and there were also great difficulties owing to Sung's inability to speak perfect English. He formed the impression that the statements Sung had made were untrue, but owing to the language problem he was not in a position to contest it. He asked the court to agree that, looking at the case as a whole, there was something in the trial which was unsatisfactory. He suggested that the detectives who had taken Sung's statements had made *bona fide* mistakes. The prisoner was a very highly strung Chinaman, and was very upset at the time. He submitted that there was misdirection by the judge regarding the weapon supposed to have caused the victim's death.

In answer, the Lord Chief Justice pointed out that there was an interpreter present at the trial and that Mr Powell KC for the prosecution, had stated that the interpreter was a 'fair and good one'. He said:

> All the evidence pointed to the complete innocence of Li Ting Jig, whom Sung had accused of committing the murder. It was clear that the first blow, the one which led to eventual death, was struck with the hammer. Every care was taken by the learned judge, and everyone else, that the trial should be perfectly fair. We have come to the conclusion, notwithstanding the careful argument addressed to us by Mr Coventry, that there are no grounds for impugning the verdict or for criticising the summing up of the learned judge.

The application for 'appeal against conviction' was then duly dismissed.

During his short confinement Sung received the ministrations of the Revd W.J. Worster, chaplain of Worcester Prison, and was converted to Christianity. On Wednesday 3 December 1919, escorted by two warders, he calmly walked from his cell to the place of execution, a converted coach house within the confines of the jail, where the scaffold had been earlier erected, calculated with a drop of 8ft 6in. The Revd Worster read the burial service as Sung was placed in position, above the trap door, by the executioner John Ellis. At the appointed time, Ellis pulled the lever and the Chinaman plunged through the aperture to his doom. The rope pulled tight around his neck and death was instantaneous.

Later, the Prison Governor ,Mr W. Young, reported to the press that 'The execution was carried out expeditiously, without a hitch, and with due solemnity.' Dr Watson, the prison doctor, confirmed that the execution was properly carried out. Sung left no statement to be read out after his death, but perhaps he saw no need to; in the pursuit of justice the puzzle of the Warley Woods murder had already been solved. Now Zee Ming Wu finally had his revenge.

# 4

# WIFE KILLING AT THE WAKES

*Willenhall, 1920*

Anyone who has served a term of imprisonment passed by a British court will undoubtedly have sampled sturdy Willenhall-made products; for this ancient township, sandwiched between larger neighbours Walsall and Wolverhampton, has long been the nucleus of the country's lockmaking industry.

It was in this skilled trade that Samuel Westwood was employed as a keysmith at Levi Poole & Sons factory in Lane Head, residing with his parents, Samuel senior and Edna, nearby at the family home in Bentley Lane, Short Heath.

During the First World War he had served the country for three years with the South Staffordshire Regiment. On 21 March 1918, while on outpost duty at Bullecourt, France, he was wounded when a shell exploded yards away, killing a sergeant and two privates. He was afterwards taken prisoner and remained in German hands until the armistice, when he was liberated and demobbed from the Army.

In November 1919, he met Miss Lydia Vaughan, a pretty young woman, also employed in the lock trade as a varnisher at David Beard & Sons Anchor Works in Cemetery Road. She was the eldest daughter of George and Annie Vaughan, who lived in Cross Street, right in the centre of the bustling town. Of two sisters and two brothers, one of the latter was 'Toddy' Vaughan, a former Willenhall Town FC player who had recently signed to Bristol Rovers.

As their romance developed, Samuel began to exhibit a worrying possessiveness for his sweetheart, one day warning her shocked father, 'If I don't have her, nobody else shall,' before adding the chilling words, 'I will do her in and then do myself in afterwards.' Mr Vaughan must have felt a great unease when only six weeks later,

*Market Place, Willenhall, a town renowned for the manufacture of locks and keys. (Courtesy of Michael Glasson)*

on 31 July 1920 the couple were married, the bride aged twenty-four years and the groom aged twenty-six.

With no home of their own, the newlyweds moved in with Samuel's parents at Bentley Lane, which proved to be a great disappointment for the young wife. Her mother visited once a week, on which occasions Lydia complained bitterly that she could not get on with her in-laws. Only once during the union did Samuel visit the Vaughan household with Lydia. The marriage was a complete disaster.

On Monday 6 September, Lydia called on her mother, telling her that although she could get on with Samuel, his parents were always interfering in their affairs, and this greatly irritated her husband. She said she was afraid that she would have to part with her spouse because she could not put up with the situation much longer. Her mother, although sympathetic, persuaded her to try to tolerate her in-laws a little more while she had to live with them, reminding her that she had only been wed for a short time.

However, the following Thursday morning, she received a message from her daughter, begging to return to her childhood home. When she arrived at the Westwood household shortly after 8 a.m., a tearful Lydia told her, 'They have been on with me all night, and his mother and father have told me to go.' Mrs Vaughan began to help pack her daughter's clothes, whilst the Westwoods protested that she did not know how to cook for their son, to wash, nor do anything for him. As the young woman left the house, suitcase in hand, she passed her husband as he made his way to the breakfast table, but not a word was exchanged. That afternoon, Lydia arranged to start back in her old job at the Anchor Works, which she had given up to become a housewife.

*Lydia Westwood. (Courtesy of Dudley Archives and Local History Service)*

*Samuel Westwood. (Courtesy of Dudley Archives and Local History Service)*

Willenhall Wakes was traditionally held to coincide with the Feast of St Giles, to whom the parish church, standing close by the entrance to the Wakes Ground in Walsall Street, is dedicated. On the morning of the wake gathering, Saturday 11 September, Lydia received a letter from her brother in Bristol, who was very fond of his eldest sister, urging her not to return to her husband, a request she would fatally ignore later that day.

During the afternoon she accompanied her parents on a journey to Walsall, returning to Willenhall about 8 p.m. Knowing it was likely Samuel would be at the funfair held on the Wake Ground, she declared that she would go there to talk things over with him. Mr Vaughan begged her not to go, exclaiming, 'If you go I shall never see you anymore until I see you a corpse. He's sure to do you in!' Despite this, the second warning that day not to fraternise with her possessive husband, she set out for the fairground, her mother insisting on accompanying her.

Mr Vaughan, meanwhile, made his way to the Prince of Wales public house, situated on the corner of Walsall Street and Church Street, a little way from the Wakes Ground.

Lydia soon spotted Samuel, and walked close to his heels all around the Wake Ground, getting nearer as they approached the exit gate. It was there that Samuel noticed the pair. 'Come on with me, Lyddie,' he beckoned. They linked arms, Mrs Vaughan doing so the other side, then all three set off along Walsall Street, Lydia walking in the centre.

'I can't go to your mother's, we can't agree. I do not see why your mother should scandalise me.' Lydia told her husband.

'I'll come with you anywhere, in lodgings or anywhere.' responded Samuel. Mrs Vaughan then intervened, saying, 'Let Lydia come with me tonight.'

'Well, I'll come down for you tomorrow, Lydia.' said Samuel to his wife. As they reached the junction with Church Street, Mrs Vaughan suggested they should all join her husband in the Prince of Wales adjacent. At that, Samuel tried to pull Lydia away, Mrs Vaughan pulling on her daughter's other arm in resistance.

Suddenly, without warning, Samuel placed his left arm around Lydia's neck, then pulled something from his pocket. He raised his right arm high above his head. In a swift silent motion, he brought it down again, his hand connecting with Lydia's throat. She fell to the ground in an instant. Samuel threw the item from his hand. Mrs Vaughan picked it up. It was a small pocket knife, the blade of which was bloodstained. She turned back to her daughter, slumped by the roadside. Blood gushed from a deep knife wound that had penetrated the right side of her throat. Walking close behind the trio was Mrs Maria Jukes from nearby Russell Street. Horrified by what she had just witnessed, she cried out 'Murder!', attracting the attention of other pedestrians walking to and from the fairground.

The assailant turned and ran back along Walsall Street until he reached the police station, where he made up his mind to hand himself in. In the station yard, he approached Police Constable Brown and declared, 'I have just stabbed my wife. She is down the road. I believe I have killed her.' Constable Brown led Westwood to the charge room, where Sergeant Evans was on duty. 'Sergeant, this man has just come to me in the yard and told me that he has stabbed his wife down the road, and he thinks he has killed her.' reported the constable.

Westwood was placed in the custody of Constable Wild, while Sergeant Evans and Constable Brown hurried from the station and along Walsall Street. By now, a large crowd had gathered around the stricken Mrs Vaughan and her collapsed daughter. They found Lydia lying on her back. She bled profusely from her injury, a pool of crimson blood forming around her in the roadway. Sergeant Evans plugged the wound with his handkerchief. Mrs Vaughan closed shut the pocket knife and handed it to Constable Brown, saying, 'He has murdered my daughter with it.' Constable Brown examined the weapon and noticed that the bloodied blade had been recently sharpened on both upper and lower edges. A bystander was summoned to fetch Dr Dean, while in the meantime, the two officers carried the lifeless woman back to the police station, the doctor arriving at practically the same time. As the clock struck 9 p.m., the doctor declared life to be extinct.

Meanwhile, in the charge room, whilst searching Westwood's pockets, Constable Wild found a small paper envelope containing white powder. Immediately, Westwood spoke, 'I've taken poison,' he declared. Constable Wild asked what he had taken. 'Some out of that packet,' he said, pointing to the envelope. When asked what the substance was, he replied, 'Some stuff I have taken from where I work. It is used

*The Prince of Wales public house, Walsall Street, Willenhall. The corner of Church Street, where Lydia Westwood collapsed dying, is seen in the foreground. (Author's collection)*

for the hardening of tools.' Dr Dean was urgently consulted, and administered an emetic to the young man to induce vomiting.

At 10 p.m., with Westwood showing no signs of ill-effect, he told Constable Wild:

> She left me last Thursday. I intended to do it the first time I saw her. I had a few pints of beer or I could not have done it. They thought I was too frightened to do it, but I have shown them. She was awkward, and I was awkward. Two awkward people do not get on together. We would have been alright if they had left us alone.

When Sergeant Evans read the charge that Westwood did 'wilfully murder his wife', he simply replied, 'Yes.'

On Monday morning, 13 September, Westwood was put before local magistrates, Messrs S. Lister JP and J.R. Mattock JP. Slight in stature, although with a soldierly appearance, he seemed quite composed when the charge was put to him that he had murdered his wife the previous Saturday evening. He seemed to treat the affair with the utmost nonchalance.

Superintendent Tucker informed the Bench that he only intended offering formal evidence to justify a remand. He then applied for an adjournment of seven days, explaining that in the meantime, the Director of Public Prosecutions would be communicated with, and would probably be represented at the next hearing.

At the inquest into the death of his wife, held that afternoon, Westwood was also present, again exhibiting a perfectly calm demeanour.

Evidence of identification was given by Mr George Vaughan, Lydia's father. He said he last saw his daughter alive on the evening of Saturday 11 September, when she was preparing to go out to the funfair on the Wakes Ground to seek her husband. He begged her not to go, his reason being that previous to their marriage, Westwood had threatened to 'do Lydia in' if she ever left him.

The county coroner, Mr J.T. Higgs, told Westwood that he was entitled to ask witnesses any questions he liked on the evidence they produced. He suggested it would be perhaps better if he did not do so at the moment as he was not yet represented by a solicitor. No doubt he would be represented later on.

Westwood said he would like to ask Mr Vaughan if he actually heard him say he would 'do Lydia in'. Mr Vaughan replied that he actually heard him say it when both were stood on the doorstep of the family home in Cross Street. 'You are here to speak the truth,' spat Westwood.

'That is the truth,' retaliated Mr Vaughan.

Dr H.J. Dean said that he was called to examine the deceased about 9 p.m. that Saturday. When he arrived she was already dead. She had a wound 1½in deep by the side of her windpipe, in the region of the big blood vessels. Death was due to haemorrhage. When he saw Westwood later that evening, he was quite calm and not under the influence of alcohol.

The coroner's jury returned a verdict of 'Wilful Murder' against Westwood. Then, at this own request, he was allowed to view the body of his wife.

At Willenhall police court on Monday 20 September, Westwood was represented by solicitor Mr Ernest J. Hall. Mr H.J. Parnham appeared for the Director of Public Prosecutions.

George Vaughan again repeated the threat Westwood had made to 'do Lydia in'. Cross-examined by Mr Hall, he said that only himself and the prisoner were present when the threat was made, but he was quite sure it was said. The interrogation continued:

*Mr Hall:* 'What objection had you to the wedding?'
*Mr Vaughan:* 'I had no objection whatever.'
*Mr Hall:* 'Did he come to you and ask for permission to marry your daughter?'
*Mr Vaughan:* 'Yes.'
*Mr Hall:* 'What did you say?'
*Mr Vaughan:* 'I said that as they made their own bed, they must lie on it, the same as I did.'
*Mr Hall:* 'Do you think a wife's place in with her husband?'
*Mr Vaughan:* 'I cannot answer that question.'

Mr Hall was equally as awkward when cross-examining Annie Vaughan.

*Mr Hall:* 'Why did you try to pull your daughter away from her husband?'

*Mrs Vaughan:* 'I wanted her to go with me.'

*Mr Hall:* 'Why did you want her to go?'

*Mrs Vaughan:* 'I had a funny sensation come over me, and said "Lydia, come with me".'

*Mr Hall:* 'Westwood begged very hard for his wife to go with him, did he not?'

*Mrs Vaughan:* 'I did not hear him.'

*Mr Hall:* 'Westwood loved your daughter, did he not?'

*Mrs Vaughan:* 'The way he used to come and see her, I thought he did.'

*Mr Hall:* 'You have never heard him threaten her, have you?'

*Mrs Vaughan:* 'No.'

*Mr Hall:* 'Have you always found him to be a quiet young man?'

*Mrs Vaughan:* 'He has never done anything to me.'

*Mr Hall:* 'When he asked your daughter to go with him, do you remember saying: "You are not going back"?'

*Mrs Vaughan:* 'No; I said, "Come with me tonight".'

When giving evidence, Edna Westwood stood up protectively for her son saying:

> They seemed to go on alright, and my husband and me had nothing to do with them. Lydia, however, was not contented. The house did not suit her, although she and Samuel had the front bedroom to themselves. We did everything we could to make them comfortable. The night before she left, they quarrelled in bed. Next morning, my son told me she was 'on at him all night over money'. He had been giving her £4 a week, but could not spare that much the last time because of bills that had to be paid. The result was she left him that Thursday. Samuel was a good steady boy. He was very upset when he found his wife had gone away.

Mr Hall applied to the Bench for a certificate for the prisoner to obtain legal assistance under the 'Poor Prisoner's Defence Act'. He said that Westwood's parents were old age pensioners who were absolutely without means. The Magistrate's Clerk, Mr Samuel Mills Slater, pointed out that under the terms of the act, the nature of the prisoner's defence must be stated otherwise the magistrates had no power to issue a certificate. Mr Hall replied that under those circumstances, he would disclose his defence. It would be insanity, and he had ample proof of that plea.

However, when defending barrister, Mr T.P. Haslam, used that plea on the prisoner's behalf at Stafford Assizes on Friday 19 November 1920, the desired result was not attained. Mr Haslam asked the jury to accept that, whilst under provocation, Westwood had committed the offence whilst his mind was temporarily unbalanced, and without malice they should return a lesser verdict of manslaughter.

The defence's case was damned when Mr J. Lort Williams, prosecuting, produced Dr Hamblin Smith, medical officer of Winson Green Prison, who stated that he had examined the defendant and found him to be quite sane.

*Magistrate's Clerk, Mr Samuel Mills Slater. (Author's collection)*

The jury retired at 4.25 p.m., taking only fifteen minutes to return their verdict, 'guilty of wilful murder.' Westwood remained quite unmoved as the judge passed sentence of death in the usual form.

Samuel Westwood was executed on the gallows at Winson Green Prison on Thursday 30 December 1920.

# 5

# A BIZARRE MESSAGE

*Walsall, 1920*

Famed as the 'Leathergoods Capital' of the British Isles, Walsall, located to the extreme north-east of the Black Country, is one of the region's larger and more ancient borough towns. In the wake of the First World War, which had brought great wealth through huge military contracts for their trusted and durable equestrian products, many of Walsall's saddlemakers exhibited at the 1920 British Industries Fair, showcasing their growing sideline in various light leathergoods, such as belts, purses and wallets.

Later that year, one of the most gruesome domestic tragedies to ever occur in the annals of the town, was discovered in the early hours of Wednesday 24 November, at the Athenaeum Buildings, Lower Bridge Street.

Police Constables Taylor and Lewis were on town-centre patrol, when they heard a loud report, which they took to be the violent slamming of a door, come from the living quarters above the premises of Sidney William Derry, barber and tobacconist. Raised voices also emanated from the property, those of a male and female engaged in a furious quarrel, although it could not be discerned what was being said.

Two and a half hours later, at 3.30 a.m., whilst examining the doors of the Imperial Picture House, situated in nearby Darwall Street, Police Constable Taylor heard the crashing of glass, followed by a heavy thud, come from the tiny rear yard of Derry's shop, which was only separated from the back premises of the cinema by a narrow service road and the open course of Walsall Brook.

The officer straddled the brook and climbed the dividing wall to Derry's yard. He was joined by Inspector Cooke and Constable Lewis, who had vaulted the boundary wall of the London City and Midland Bank, which also abutted onto the premises. There, the three policemen discovered Sidney Derry lying huddled up in a pool of blood near to a small wooden shed. He wore only his shirt and trousers, and one sock. Although semi-conscious, and with a wound to the throat, he attempted

to stand up several times, but only fell back down again. High above them an attic window was propped fully open. Evidently, Derry had fallen a great height, his descent being broken by first landing on the shed roof, on which had been stored a sheet of plate glass.

Dr Godfrey Baker was sent for from his Bradford Street surgery. On arrival, he rendered first aid to Derry's throat injury, a severe cut which appeared to have been self-inflicted. The patient was then conveyed by ambulance to Walsall General Hospital. With the drama now over, it was noticed that the remaining occupants of the premises had apparently slept undisturbed throughout. The police pounded both the front and back doors, but still there was no response. It was then decided to force an entry, the circumstances being sinister as they were.

Police Constable Taylor entered through a rear window into an anteroom at the back of the hairdressing salon. Immediately, he noticed a strong smell of gas. The constable admitted Inspector Cooke and Constable Lewis to the building, who were also joined by Dr Baker. Everything seemed in order throughout the ground-floor shop premises. With the aid of a small electric torch, Inspector Cooke led the way upstairs where the family pet dog was found roaming about the rooms.

*Rear of Sidney Derry's tobacconist shop,*
*showing the top-floor window from which*
*he fell. (Author's collection)*

The four investigators passed through the first floor sitting room, whose bay window overlooked the neat shop front below, and out into the rear kitchen situated above the hairdressing salon. There it became clear where the overpowering smell of gas was issuing from. All the oven burners were turned fully on, but unlit. The main oven door lay open and inside was a bloodstained folded bedsheet. Windows were urgently opened to expel the dangerous substance, and the taps to the appliance turned safely off. On the kitchen table stood a pint bottle containing a small quantity of rum.

Continuing their search, the men entered the second-floor front bedroom, where the scanty light from Inspector Cooke's now failing torch revealed an awful tragedy. The room contained two double beds. On one lay Derry's two young daughters, both with their throats gashed and bullet wounds to the head. The younger girl, Gwendoline Annie, aged three years was quite dead, but her sister, Irene Clara, aged six, showed signs of life. She was at once wrapped in a blanket and carried away to hospital by Police Constable Taylor.

The other bed was saturated with blood. Underneath, clothed in her blood-drenched nightdress and lying face upwards, was found the body of Derry's wife of six years, Emma, aged thirty-one. Her throat had been horribly cut from ear to ear. In addition, she bore gunshot wounds to the head and chest. A bloodied razor lay on the floor alongside the body.

Gas issued from a bracket wrenched from the wall. Constable Taylor found where the meter was installed, but the key to close down the supply was missing, so a spanner was sent for from the fire station, with which to do the job.

With Inspector Cooke's torch now exhausted, it was decided to suspend the search of the premises until daybreak. The bodies of the unfortunate wife and daughter were conveyed to the town mortuary, situated in Wolverhampton Street, and the family pet dog taken to the animal pound. A solitary policeman was left standing guard over the property throughout the remainder of the night.

At 7.45 a.m., Inspector Cooke and Constable Taylor returned to the crime scene, accompanied with Chief Inspector Ballance, to resume their investigations. Between the two beds was found another bloodstained cut-throat razor, and nearby lay a small

*Sidney Derry's tobacconist shop, Lower Bridge Street, the morning after the triple tragedy. The bodies were discovered in the front bedroom, seen with the paired sash windows. (Courtesy of Walsall Local History Centre)*

*Emma Derry. (Courtesy of Walsall Local History Centre)*

nickel-plated six-chambered revolver, still fully loaded. On the mantelpiece was a box labelled 'Fifty Kynoch .32' containing six more live rounds, whilst a total of seven other spent cartridges littered the bedroom floor.

Upon a small bedside table, Inspector Cooke discovered a piece of notepaper, on which was scrawled a bizarre message. It read:

> Let anyone keep clear of such a viper as —, or
> —, of — Street, manager of the — Company,
> — Street who is the biggest liar and cunning
> rogue; Also the —'s of Walsall, — and his cross-
> eyed friend —; Otherwise they will find themselves
> as I have done. They are nothing but a pack of rogues
> and thieves.

Was this an intended suicide note written by a man acting under great duress?

The investigating trio followed a trail of blood up a narrow flight of stairs to the fourth-storey attic room. There, a third bloodstained razor rested on the inside window ledge. It could be safely assumed that Derry had attempted to gas himself, but failing to do so had then cut his own throat, before plummeting from the attic window, his fall being broken by the wooden shed 28ft below. Further searches produced two more soiled razors, one on the kitchen hearth rug, and the other folded inside the blankets of the children's bed, making a total of five of the bloodstained lethal implements being found.

Would-be customers were greeted with a notice posted on the shop door in Lower Bridge Street, stating only that the premises were closed. However, with Derry being such a familiar figure in the busy town centre, word of the awful tragedy soon spread around the district.

Sidney William Derry had served in the Royal Naval Division in France during the latter part of the First World War, being chiefly involved in transport work and the burying of the dead. The twenty-nine-year-old, whose parents lived in Raleigh Street, had married his wife, formerly Miss Perkins of Hospital Street, in February 1914 at St Paul's Church in the town, thereafter establishing their successful business, of which Emma was in charge of tobacco sales. Derry was also well known in sporting circles, although his vice was gambling on the racehorses.

When interviewed by the *Walsall Observer* newspaper, Derry's father said that since his son was demobilized from the Navy two years previously, he seemed slightly

*Gwendoline Annie Derry. (Courtesy of Walsall Local History Centre)*

absent minded and had been frequently unwell. That evening, the headlines revealed that both Derry and little Irene, lay in their hospital beds in a serious condition. Meanwhile, post-mortem examinations were carried out by Dr Baker on the bodies of Mrs Derry and her younger daughter. Throughout the night, two policemen guarded Derry on his hospital ward, whilst others prevented anyone from entering the back premises of his shop, from which officials had already removed a quantity of cash and personal jewellery for safekeeping.

'The greatest tragedy that has occurred for many, many years in Walsall, and certainly one that has sent a thrill of horror throughout the whole community' was how the borough coroner, James Flockhart Addison, described the terrible affair as he opened the inquests at the Guildhall, in the High Street, on Friday 26 November. The only formal evidence taken was from Miss Ellen Perkins, of Hospital Street, who had identified the bodies of her sister and niece at the mortuary.

*The Guildhall, High Street, Walsall, with former police station to the right. (Author's collection)*

*James Flockhart Addison, Walsall Borough Coroner, 1920. (Author's collection)*

She stated that for the past thirteen months, she had worked as an assistant at the shop, arriving at 8.30 a.m. daily, sometimes Sunday included, and leaving about 9 p.m. She last saw her niece alive at 8 p.m. on the Wednesday when she put both girls to bed. When she left the premises at 8.45 p.m., her sister was also alive and well, sitting reading by the fireplace, alongside her husband. Afterwards, the coroner adjourned the hearing, giving the jurors instructions to return at 3 p.m. on Monday 6 December.

Since the passing of the Wartime Act, the empanelling of a jury by a coroner had been a rare occurrence. However, having regard to the serious nature of the case, Mr Addison took the decision to revert back to the old practice.

The joint funerals of Mrs Derry and Gwendoline were held at Ryecroft Cemetery, Walsall, on Monday 29 November, a sad spectacle witnessed by upwards of 3,000 townspeople. A large crowd gathered in pouring rain to see the cortège leave the Perkins family home in Hospital Street, many following the funeral coaches down Proffitt Street and Coalpool Lane to the cemetery gates. Here, two stalwart policemen watched the long line of mourners trudge the sodden pathway to the neat cemetery chapel, where the Revd Charles Edward McCreery, of St Peter's Church, read the first half of the burial service.

It was a touching scene as the two polished oak coffins were conveyed to the graveside, preceded by the clergyman, prayer book in hand, his head adorned with a biretta, and clothed in a white gown. Missing from the many family mourners who followed behind, were the mothers of both the deceased woman and her injured husband.

Rain pattered on the coffin lids as the Revd McCreery read aloud the committal sentences. The mother was lowered first to her final resting place, a chorus of sobs breaking the solemn silence as her daughter's tiny casket was placed above. Relatives took a last look of the open grave, then, overcome with grief, made their way back to the waiting funeral coaches.

Afterwards, there was a rush by the crowds to view the internment, but the boards were placed over so none was able to see within. As the rain continued to fall relentlessly, others inspected a beautiful array of floral tributes, including one in the form of a harp, sent by the residents of Hospital Street and the surrounding locality.

*Irene Clara Derry. (Courtesy of Walsall Local History Centre)*

It was reported from the hospital that Derry underwent an operation on Thursday 2 December, and that subsequently, his condition began to improve. The following day, at the same institution, surgery was performed on his surviving daughter, Irene, to remove a bullet lodged in her skull. Despite this, the poor girl remained in a coma and succumbed to her horrific injuries three days later at 10.54 p.m. on Monday 6 December. An inquest was opened and adjourned at the hospital by the coroner on the following Thursday morning. Three more adjournments were made before the full inquest on all three deaths was held at the hospital boardroom on, Monday 3 January 1921.

The coroner, Mr Addison, heard from Derry's solicitor, Mr Frank Platt, that on this occasion, his client would be present, as was his right. In a few minutes, the accused appeared, leaning on the arm of a police officer, as, with faltering steps, he ambled into the room. It was at once noticed that the man was now a physical wreck, his clothes hanging loosely from his thin frame, shoulders hunched, he looked almost too weak to stand. He was closely followed by Dr G. Millicent Fox, house surgeon at the hospital where he had received much medical treatment, who was careful to see that her patient was sat near to the fireplace.

Evidence of identification of all three victims was repeated by Miss Ellen Perkins, sister of Mrs Derry, who was then questioned by Mr Platt. 'Had you noticed that your brother-in-law had been moody for some time?' he asked.

'Yes,' she replied, 'He was a bit quiet.'

*Lower Bridge Street, Walsall, c. 1920. Sidney Derry's property is to the left of the tram. (Author's collection)*

'Was he worried about his business?' queried the solicitor.

'Yes, he was worried because he could not get enough stock,' answered the woman.

Mr Frederick Smith, of Thelma Street, Palfrey, said that since Easter 1919, he had been employed as a hairdressing assistant by Derry. He recalled the afternoon of Tuesday 23 November, the previous year, when Derry was away from the shop delivering orders for his wholesale tobacco round, which he covered by bicycle. Shortly after his return, he ate evening dinner with his wife before returning to the salon until closing time at 8 p.m. Mr Smith insisted that Derry seemed his normal self that day, except that he had been run down a little with a common cold.

Mr Harry Perkins, brother-in-law of the accused, a baker living at the family home in Hospital Street, told of last speaking to his sister at about 7.30 p.m. the same day at the Lower Bridge Street shop. Derry asked him to wait until he had finished in the salon, then joined him to walk up Park Street shortly after 8 p.m. Outside Her Majesty's Theatre, his brother-in-law spoke to a man named Joseph Cockayne, who Mr Perkins had earlier seen in Derry's shop. Derry then went to take a tobacco order from a customer in Wolverhampton Street, while he himself went in the oyster bar at the theatre.

Later, they met together again and called at the Prince Blucher Inn, Stafford Street, where they drank two half pints of beer each. After staying about fifteen minutes, Derry purchased a pint bottle of old ale to take away, then called at Garfield's cook shop for a pork sandwich, which he said was for his wife's supper. A little after 8.30 p.m., they wished each other 'goodnight' and parted company. Mr Perkins also observed that Derry appeared his normal convivial self. Mr Platt asked, 'Do you know that your brother-in-law has lost a considerable amount of money gambling on the racing horses. Did he ever tell you so?'

'Not that I remember,' replied the surprised man.

Police Inspector Cooke informed the panel of jurors of the events leading to the discovery of the carnage in the flat above Derry's business, producing the nickel-plated revolver and five bloodstained razors as he spoke. Fingering the razors, he pointed out how two of them had been splintered, some of the steel fragments having been found in the children's bed. Chief Inspector Ballance added that such cutting edges were easily broken, especially when they came into contact with bone!

Next, the inquiry heard the results of the post-mortems, carried out on the bodies of Emma Derry and her youngest daughter, Gwendoline, by Dr Baker, on Thursday 25 November.

Starting with the injuries to Mrs Derry's right hand, he said there was a strip of flesh, 1½in long, cut from the inside of the thumb. On the second finger was an incised wound measuring just under an inch, with a smaller cut over the middle joint of the third finger. These, he felt, were defensive injuries. There were no marks on the left hand. Four deep gashes encircled three quarters of the circumference of the victim's neck, penetrating through its structures to the vertebral column. The thyroid cartilage had been cut through, the incision reaching almost to the root of the tongue. More fragments of steel blade were found in these wounds.

On examining the skull, he found that halfway between the right eye and ear was a circle of brown charring, indicating a gun having been fired at close quarters. The bullet had traversed the under-surface of the brain and slightly lacerated it, before coming to rest in the right temple bone.

Another bullet had entered the chest, first passing clean through the sixth rib, then along the stomach before penetrating the liver and diaphragm. This projectile was discovered in the right pleural cavity. The doctor thought that, considering the defensive wounds to the right hand, death was due to extensive throat injuries, the bullets having been fired later.

Speaking of the autopsy on the child, Gwendoline, he found two gaping wounds in the neck, each about 1½in long, and 1in wide at the centre. Her tiny skull bore three bullet wounds. Two had entered through the left temple, and another behind the left ear. When the cranium was opened up for examination, one of the bullets fell from the cavity and rolled along the cold mortuary slab. The second bullet had embedded itself 2in inwards, behind the left ear, whilst the third floated around in the lacerated soft tissue of the child's brain. In this instance, death was undoubtedly caused by the gunshot wounds.

The post-mortem on the third victim, Irene, was carried out by Dr Fox, assisted by Dr Deakin, on the instructions of the coroner, at the hospital where the child had been treated. She was found to have two superficial wounds to the neck, each about 4in in length, and another measuring 2in, which was much deeper, underneath her chin.

There was a blackened and charred bullet wound to the right temple, which had also singed the little girl's hair, indicating the shot had been fired at very close range. The bullet had passed through the brain to the left temple, where it rebounded, passing back through the brain again, before coming to rest in the bone of the skull. Death was due to inflammation of the brain tissue. Dr Fox revealed that when the child was admitted to the hospital, a stray bullet had dropped from her clothing during the initial assessment of her injuries.

Throughout the harrowing disclosures made during the post-mortem reports, Derry remained unmoved. Wearing a stiff collar and tie over his bandaged neck, his head tilted to the left, he stared blankly ahead, occasionally glancing at his in-laws, but showing no recognition of either. It was impossible to judge whether he was following proceedings.

Summing up the evidence, the coroner advised the jury that there seemed little doubt that Derry had inflicted the throat wounds and discharged the bullets into all three victims. Speaking in solemn tones, he told them:

> You can come to no other conclusion than Emma Derry died at the hands of her husband, and Gwendoline and Irene died at the hands of their father. Whether he knew what he was doing at the time these unlawful acts were committed is not for you to say. That is a matter for another jury.

Following a short deliberation, the foreman, Mr I. Genders, announced that the jury found Derry responsible for all three deaths. Addressing the perpetrator, who sat with his head bowed, the coroner said, 'I don't know whether you have understood the verdict of the jury, but they find you guilty of three counts of murder, and it is my duty, as a coroner, to commit you upon those charges to take your trial in due course.' Even then, Derry gazed dreamily on, seemingly unable to appreciate the terrible accusation against him: triple murder!

On Wednesday 12 January, Derry was brought before the magistrates for a remand hearing. Looking very unwell, he was aided slowly to the dock, where, after glancing around the court for a moment, he slumped backwards, apparently too weak to stand erect. Despite this, it was declared that he was to be discharged from hospital and removed to Winson Green Prison, Birmingham, to await his trial.

He appeared much the same when remanded again by the magistrates the following Wednesday, his throat still swathed in bandages, hidden beneath a fawn-coloured raincoat with the collar turned up. The Chief Constable, Mr A. Thomson, intimated that by the following week, a representative from the Department of Public Prosecutions would be available to proceed with the case.

This, the committal hearing, took place at the Guildhall on Wednesday 26 January. Prosecuting for the Crown was Mr Ross Pashley, while Derry was once again defended by his solicitor, Mr Frank Platt. Mr R.T. Jupp JP was the presiding magistrate, and the Magistrate's Clerk, Mr S.E. Loxton.

The prisoner was brought from Winson Green by train to Walsall station, and then by car to the police cells. He entered the court a forlorn figure, a fresh growth of dark beard emphasising the paleness of his skin. Mr Platt asked that his client might be allowed a seat in the dock, the justices readily agreeing.

In his opening statement, Mr Pashley described Derry as a 'racing man', who had frequently attended race meetings for the purpose of bookmaking, suggesting, 'Bookmakers usually have plenty of money, and this, coupled with the fact that £132 was found on the premises, shows that the man was in no financial difficulty.' Mr Platt, however, challenged this, alleging that he had, in fact, lost several hundred pounds on the races and had an outstanding claim against him.

Mr Pashley suggested there was much evidence of premeditation in the crime, saying:

> Five cut throat razors had been taken from the hairdressing salon below, along with the nickel-plated revolver, all of which had been used to inflict the terrible injuries, and were found in various locations in the living quarters. Not satisfied with cutting their throats, he then finished off all three victims with the revolver, reloading the weapon when it became empty.

During examination of Derry's sister-in-law, Miss Ellen Perkins, Mr Pashley produced the nickel-plated revolver, asking, 'Have you seen this before?'

'Yes, it belongs to my late sister's husband', she replied.

'Prior to 23 November 1920, where was it kept?', asked the solicitor. Miss Perkins explained that it was usually to be found in a drawer beneath the shop counter, where the takings from the hairdressing salon were kept.

Mr Pashley then took the bizarrely worded notepaper, found in the bedroom, and showed it to the witness. 'Do you know the prisoner's handwriting?', he inquired.

'I think I can tell it', said Miss Perkins.

'Then look at this note and tell me whether the handwriting is the prisoner's.' instructed Mr Pashley.

'Yes, I should say it is', she confirmed.

'What is meant by the note I do not know', commented Mr Pashley.

A new witness was called to give evidence, Mr Joseph Cockayne, a toolmaker, from Prince Street, in the Pleck district of the town. He was the man who Derry's brother-in-law, Harry Perkins, had said called in the hairdressing salon and later in the evening met with the prisoner in Park Street, on Tuesday 23 November, prior to the crimes in the early hours of the following day.

He explained that he first met Derry six months before, while journeying to Warwick August Races. They travelled in the same motor car, became quite friendly, and attended several more race meetings together. Derry made a book and Cockayne did the clerking. At the end of the Liverpool meeting, last November, Derry had £25 winnings on the book.

Mr Cockayne agreed that he called in Derry's shop on 23 November and later approached him in Park Street. 'Did you speak to him in connection with racing?' asked Mr Pashley.

'Yes', answered the witness.

'Did he appear to be his usual self?', probed the solicitor.

'I thought he seemed slightly agitated. I asked him if he was going to Manchester Races on the following Thursday. He replied, "I don't know, Joe, I haven't decided yet. Will you call round and see me in the morning?" I called as he asked, but of course could not see him', was the lengthy reply.

Cross-examining, Mr Platt asked, 'Do you know whether Derry had lost a lot of money on the horses?'

'No', replied Mr Cockayne, 'but I do believe he did a lot more betting in addition to the bookmaking.'

'Don't you know he had lost three or four hundred pounds?', asked Mr Platt.

'Not to my knowledge', said Mr Cockayne, before reiterating, 'He used to bet apart, because I have been told about it by others.'

'Do you know that someone had a claim against him for a bet?', inquired Mr Platt.

'Yes sir', answered the witness.

'A claim you have applied for yourself?', pressed the solicitor.

'Yes sir', confirmed Mr Cockayne.

Chief Inspector Ballance, in describing the crime scene, said that the living quarters above Derry's shop contained six rooms. These consisted of a living room, sitting room, kitchen, two bedrooms and the attic room. The front bedroom, in which the tragedy occurred, measured 18ft by 13ft, and was 10ft in height. It contained two beds, a wardrobe, washstand, five chairs and two small tables.

The case for the prosecution closed just as the clock struck four in the afternoon. Now the full charge of 'triple murder and attempted suicide' was put to the prisoner by the presiding magistrate. It was then, for the first time, that Derry strove to speak. Half rising to his feet, and clutching at the bandage still encircling his throat, he made a choking noise in his endeavour to plead. His solicitor then rose on his behalf and said, 'He desires to plead not guilty and reserve his defence.'

After a short adjournment, Mr Platt conducted the case for Derry's defence. Once again, his client seemed to take little interest in the proceedings. He sat looking straight ahead, seemingly dazed and uncomprehending. It was only when the magistrates committed him to take his trial at the next Stafford Assizes, and his solicitor turned to consult him, that he appeared to realise the perilous position he was in.

Twenty-six days later, on Monday 21 February 1921, the old court chamber at Stafford was the impressive, yet sombre, setting for the final act in one of the most tragic domestic dramas that Walsall had ever known. There was all the majesty and ceremony of the law to be seen.

*Sidney William Derry's Lower Bridge Street premises today. (Author's collection)*

Punctually, at a quarter to eleven in the morning, Mr Justice Sankey appeared at the small door behind the judge's dais, resplendent in his robes of ermine and attended by the High Sheriff, immaculately dressed in velvet. There was more theatrical apparel amongst the clerk to the assize and the members of the bar, seated below in front of the broad dock, wigs and black flowing gowns aplenty. The chaplain, adorned in full ecclesiastic costume, high-ranking policemen, conspicuous with long hand-held tapering ceremonial wands, and various other uniformed court and prison officials made up a company worthy of London's greatest playhouses.

The court rose whilst the judge took his seat beneath the wooden canopy. Then came the order from the Clerk of Assize to, 'Put up Sidney William Derry.' All eyes turned to the dock. In a few minutes, the prisoner appeared, accompanied by two warders.

It was immediately apparent to those who had witnessed Derry's demeanour at previous hearings in Walsall that the passing month had brought about a great deterioration in his mental state. Trembling, his face pale and drawn, he rested his hands on the dock rail, as in faltering tones, and with great difficulty, he pleaded, 'Not guilty', as the charges were put to him. He still wore a bandage firmly around his neck, beneath the same fawn-coloured raincoat as in previous appearances.

During the swearing in of the jury, which included five women, he glanced towards his solicitor, Mr Frank Platt, who sat at the side of the dock behind his counsel for defence, Mr Graham Millward. Afterwards, he averted his gaze and looked around to that part of the court occupied by Dr G. Millicent Fox, who had overseen his medical treatment at Walsall Hospital. These were the people whom Derry was dependant on to save his neck from the gallows.

The barristers for the prosecution were Mr St John Micklethwaite and Mr Lawrence Mead. Opening the case, Mr Micklethwaite said the story was a fearful one, because not only was Derry charged with murdering three people, but that those three people were his wife and two young daughters. He told the court, 'It was one of those strange, almost unaccountable tragedies, resulting in the wiping out of a whole family.'

Of all the evidence given that day, none was more crucial to Derry's cause than that given by Dr Fox. Her degree, she said, was a Bachelor of Medicine of the Edinburgh University:

Mr Mead (for the prosecution): 'What was the prisoner's condition when he was admitted to the hospital?'

Dr Fox: 'He was acting very violently, throwing his arms and legs about, and trying to call out, but as his throat had been cut, he could not make any definite sound, although I thought I heard him say "mother".'

At this, Derry fought to contain his emotions and swayed in the dock.

Mr Mead: 'Can you form an opinion as to the state of his mind?'

Dr Fox: 'I came to the conclusion that he was maniacal at the time he was admitted.'

Mr Mead: 'Can you form an opinion as to whether he could realise the nature or consequences of the acts he had committed?'

Dr Fox: 'I do not think he had any idea of what he had done at all. That was confirmed later, because his throat was stitched at the time of admission, yet about eight days later, when it had to be done again, he wanted to know why it had not been done before.'

Mr Mead: 'You think he did not realise?'

Dr Fox: 'I think he had no idea of what had happened at the time.'

Then Mr Millward took the lead in cross-examining the lady doctor:

*Mr Millward:* 'You mean that he did not know whether he had done wrong?'

*Dr Fox:* 'I cannot say whether he knew if he had done right or wrong, but he did not seem to know what he was doing.'

*Mr Millward:* 'That means that he did not know the nature of his act?'

*Dr Fox:* 'Yes.'

*Mr Millward:* 'Was he extremely violent?'

*Dr Fox:* 'Yes, there were four men and a nurse holding him down while his throat was being stitched.'

*Mr Millward:* 'Was that necessary for almost a day after he was admitted?'

*Dr Fox:* 'Quite a day. Two policemen were constantly in the room holding him down.'

*Mr Millward:* 'Was a straightjacket needed?'

*Dr Fox:* 'Yes, the following day.'

*Mr Millward:* 'Did he continue to be violent for something like two or three days?'

*Dr Fox:* 'Yes, he had outbreaks now and then.'

*Mr Millward:* 'How long was it before the outbursts calmed down?'

*Dr Fox:* 'About the third day.'

*Mr Millward:* 'You would have no hesitation in certifying him as insane when he was admitted to hospital?'

*Dr Fox:* 'No hesitation at all.'

In summing up the case, Mr Justice Sankey said there could be no possible doubt what had happened. 'If the jury considered he was insane at the time then the law provided a very merciful verdict that a person was 'guilty but insane'. Dr Fox was in the very best position to state an opinion on that point,' he told the court. Then, referring to the jury, he added, 'I think the members can have little doubt as to what the verdict should be.'

The jury did not retire, and spent little time in consideration, before the foreman announced that they were unanimously of the opinion that the prisoner was indeed 'guilty, but insane'. The judge then made an order that the prisoner should be 'Kept in custody as a criminal lunatic until His Majesty's pleasure shall be met.'

After the judge had passed sentence, Derry, who had sobbed uncontrollably towards the end of the trial, appeared somewhat dazed, and had to be assisted to stand. His Lordship, looking concerned, remarked quietly to the warders supporting the man either side, 'Help him out, poor chap.' Derry then turned to his solicitor and made a request to be allowed to see his mother and other relatives.

When Derry had disappeared from sight, the saintly judge intimated that he had overheard the request, saying, 'When a man is sentenced, he passes out of the custody of the judge, who has no further control over him. However, I think this is a case in which the jailer ought to allow the request, of course under proper control.' In all, the trial had barely lasted three quarters of an hour.

# 6

# SLAIN OVER
# A SIXPENCE

*Lye, 1925*

Although brick manufacturers were located in most parts of the Black Country, there was a vast bed of superior fireclay at Lye, close to Stourbridge. This was used to produce furnace linings for the region's many ironworks, and crucibles for the surrounding glass industry, amongst the otherwise everyday products of the building trade. Traditionally, women were employed as brickmoulders; the work was heavy and intensive, with each 'wench' expected to produce in excess of 1,000 bricks by the end of their daily 'stint', or allotted hours.

Miss Alice Mary Rowley had been described as 'one of the smartest and prettiest girls that ever worked in a Black Country brickyard'. She actually lived on the works premises, in the stableman's cottage, No. 132 Stourbridge Road, situated within Messrs Hickman & Co. Firebrick Works, halfway between Stambermill and Hay Green.

About 1909, her widowed mother, Ellen, met and married James Checketts, employed by Hickman's as a horse driver, bringing Alice and four elder sisters to live in the brickyard, joining four step-brothers from Mr Checketts' previous marriage. Four years later, they were blessed with yet another little girl, making a grand total of ten children.

As they grew up, James Checketts' third son, Bert, developed an unhealthy interest in his younger step-sister. By the time Alice reached twenty-two years of age, in 1925, her step-brother, now twenty-four, was completely infatuated with the young woman. He would attempt to kiss her on the lips and spoke suggestively, to which, understandably, she refused to reciprocate. More sinister, he would follow her about for miles whenever she left the house, never walking alongside, but always keeping his distance.

*Alice Mary Rowley. (Courtesy of Dudley Archives and Local History Service)*

Bert Checketts was a strange one. As a young boy he often had outbursts of bad temper and threw tantrums. His father sent him to hospital, but they turned him away as being incurable. He would suddenly start to roar with laughter at seemingly nothing at all and could not be stopped. Frustrated by Alice's refusal to acknowledge his affections, he soiled her clothing, and once broke up her favourite hats, burying them in the ash bank at the brickyard.

It could not have been easy for the young woman to avoid her unwanted admirer, for although her four elder sisters as well as one of the Checketts brothers were now married and gone, there were still seven family members sharing the tiny ramshackle cottage. This made up one side of three ranges of buildings, the other two being stables and tack rooms, enclosing a small cobbled yard, where James Checketts had now resided and worked for thirty-eight years. Alice shared one bedroom with her younger sister and parents, while Bert Checketts and his two remaining brothers slept in the other. By now, the brickworks, although still trading under the name of Hickman, were owned and operated by Messrs Garratt and Co. Ltd.

Once employed by bucket manufacturers Messrs Hill and Bowler, for three years, Bert Checketts had been out of work, doing only the occasional odd job in the brickyard. A rather short, but muscular fellow, he was once described as 'simple enough, but a hard nut to get over'! On Sundays, he attended nearby St Mark's Church for early morning worship and the afternoon Bible class. His hobby was football, although he was noted for studying the form of racing horses, his tips often paying handsome dividends. Rather admirably, he was abstemious of alcohol.

On Saturday 4 July 1925, brick burner Robert Collins, of No. 13 Grange Lane, Hadcroft, was working an evening shift, when at 7.30 p.m., he heard raised voices near the Checketts' home and went to investigate. He found Bert Checketts having a furious row with Alice Rowley. The young lady appeared very distressed and complained to Mr Collins, 'I'm glad someone has come on the scene. He is on to me. He wants to borrow sixpence from me and I have not got it. He will not let me go out.' Mr Collins told Checketts, 'Get out or I shall throw you out', to which, the aggressor backed down and walked away.

*The Checketts' family home, No. 132 Stourbridge Road, Lye, which was situated within Hickman's brickyard. (Courtesy of Dudley Archives and Local History Service)*

The following day, Bert Checketts appeared to be harbouring a grudge. It was noted that he was sulking and he avoided conversation with Alice. After attending church twice, as usual, he sat down with the rest of the family for their evening meal. After the meal, Mr and Mrs Checketts went out to the Rose and Crown public house, which was situated right opposite the entrance gates to the brickyard.

At 9 p.m., Alice called on her mother to come back to the house and make her presence known. It appeared that her step-brother had once again been annoying her. Whilst in the public house, she purchased a bottle of stout to enjoy at home later. Upon Mrs Checketts entering the house, the young man immediately left and walked to the entrance gates, his step-mother following shortly behind. Not a word was exchanged between them. Bert Checketts turned and walked along Stourbridge Road in the direction of Lye Cross. Mrs Checketts then returned to her husband at the Rose and Crown, leaving Alice in the house alone, warming the bottle of stout to drink later.

That evening, Robert Collins was again working late in the brickyard, about 150yds from the Checketts home and stables. At 9.20 p.m., he heard two short screams come from the vicinity of the stables, and deciding to investigate, proceeded to head in that direction. He had not walked far when he saw Bert Checketts coming towards him from the opposite direction. When about 50yds apart, Checketts noticed the man and turned to walk back from where he came. Mr Collins noticed that Checketts shirt was heavily stained by some dark substance, but he could not clearly make out what it was. With his day's work nearly done, he returned to his labours at the ash mound.

Meanwhile, Mrs Millie Pardoe was making her way from Stourbridge railway junction to her home at No. 21 Engine Lane, Lye, having walked across the fields, then joining Stourbridge Road via the footpath running between a pair of cottages and the railway embankment. As she approached Hickman's brickyard, she could see Bert Checketts stood at the entrance gates. It was now 9.30 p.m. When she was about to walk past the gates, Checketts beckoned for her attention, excitedly blurting out, 'There's a woman in here who's cut her throat. I struggled with her and tried to save her. She has done it herself.'

Mrs Pardoe looked Checketts up and down with horror. His face and hands were dripping with blood, as were his clothes, his right shirt sleeve torn at the shoulder, the garment being ripped open at the front. He held up his hands, repeating several times, 'I am innocent.' Although very shocked, Mrs Pardoe followed him into the brickyard. 'The body is down here.' he said, leading the woman around the corner of the stable building into the cobbled yard. There, in a massive pool of blood, lay the horrifically mutilated body of Alice Rowley, who, though well known to Mrs Pardoe, the numbed woman at first failed to recognise, such was the extent of her injuries.

Checketts continued, 'We were in the house together. She went to the drawer and took out a razor. It was my new razor that I bought only last week. I ran after her and struggled with her. She then fell on me. That is how the blood got on me. I kicked the razor from her hand.' Then pointing to cuts on his fingers, he exclaimed, 'Look how she has served me out!'

*The spot where Alice Rowley lay dead in the stableyard (marked with an 'X'). (Courtesy of Dudley Archives and Local History Service)*

Just then, Mr and Mrs Checketts arrived from the Rose and Crown, after being alerted by a brickyard worker that Bert had been seen wandering around covered in blood. As soon as she saw the body, Mrs Checketts screamed hysterically before collapsing to the ground. She got back to her feet and viewed the injuries more closely, screaming, 'My Alice! My Alice!' This alerted Robert Collins, who, shovel still in hand, left the ash mound and ran to the awful scene. Now quite a crowd began to assemble, with virtually all the customers from the Rose and Crown crossing over to the brickyard.

Bert Checketts appeared to be the most calm and collected person, amongst all who stood around the poor woman's body, awaiting the arrival of the police. He fetched a glass of cold water from the house to help restore his stricken step-mother, who was afterwards carried to the house by Robert Collins and other concerned brickyard employees. His father glanced at him and asked, 'Have you done this?', to which he replied, 'No, father, her's done it herself. I am innocent', before entering the house.

Shortly, Police Constable Gerald Dadge arrived, summoned from Lye police station. He parted the ever-growing crowd of sightseers, who formed a ring several deep around the gruesome spectacle, and observed the condition of the victim's body. She lay on her back, about 3yds from the inside corner of the stableyard, her head inclined towards the house, situated across the opposite side. He noticed a very deep wound at the back of the neck, and a gaping wound to the throat. Another massive wound had slashed open her right breast. The woman was fully clothed, her apparel, as well as her uncovered head and hands, were saturated with blood from top to toe.

Bert Checketts came running from the house and approached the sickened police officer. Noticing that he too was saturated with blood, the lawman enquired, 'What is this then?' Checketts replied, 'I am innocent. I am innocent. She did it herself. I tried to take the razor from her, and I managed to get it out of her hands.' Constable Dadge looked around. A heavily bloodstained razor lay on the cobbled surface, about 11yds away from the horribly cut up body. Police reinforcements were telephoned for from the brickyard office. Constable Dodge took custody of Checketts and detained him at Lye police station, following the arrival of Sergeant Henning.

At 9.55 p.m., Dr H.C. Darby, of Lye, arrived and began the necessary examination of the body. Her face and clothing at the front were smeared with soil and ashes from the surface of the yard, suggesting that sometime during the frenzied attack she had been turned over. Although her dress was open, it appeared that her underskirt had not been disturbed. Almost an hour later, the doctor was joined by Deputy Chief Constable T.W. Hill, who was accompanied by Inspector Frank Halford. The Deputy Chief Constable surveyed the carnage. Although now dimly lit, it could be seen that the body lay about 18yds from the entrance to the house. Satisfied that a thorough search of the crime scene would have to wait until the following morning, Deputy Chief Constable Hill ordered Sergeant Nash to oversee the body's removal to Stourbridge Mortuary.

By now, the awful news had spread far and wide, and the crowd of morbid sightseers had grown to considerably over 1,000 persons. Outside the brickyard, Stourbridge Road, usually deserted at that time on a Sunday night, was quite impassable. Another hour would go by before the crowds had dispersed and any semblance of normality was restored.

Deputy Chief Constable Hill and Inspector Halford left the brickyard and travelled the short distance to Lye police station. There, he told Bert Checketts that he was making enquiries in connection with the death of Alice Rowley. Checketts simply protested, 'I am innocent.' He stood before the two officers, caked in dried and congealed blood from top to bottom. His shirt was torn open at the front and the collar missing. The left sleeve was saturated with blood and torn in three places at the shoulder. The right sleeve had been completely torn away. His face also was covered in dried blood, with a long smear running from his left ear to the back of his neck.

The officers removed Checketts by motor car to Stourbridge police station, where Dr Darby was summoned to carry out a medical examination of the detained man. He found that Checketts' left hand and forearm were coated with blood from the fingertips to the elbow. There were also two cuts to the index finger of his left hand. The right hand was covered with blood from the fingertips to just above the wrist and another cut was found on the little finger. The doctor consulted with the two officers before leaving the station.

Checketts was removed to the charge room, where Deputy Chief Constable Hill cautioned the man before charging him with the wilful murder of Alice Mary Rowley. Once again, Checketts declared, 'I am innocent', before making the following statement:

> I was reading the *Empire News*. The young lady went to the drawer and pulled it open, then shut it closed again. She went out and walked across the yard. I happened to look through the window and saw her using the razor. She cut herself in three or four places, and I thought it was my duty to go and try to save her. That's all.

Checketts was shown the razor, a hollow ground implement with a white handle, which Constable Dadge had recovered from the stableyard floor, and asked to identify its owner. He answered 'Yes, it is mine. I bought it new at Cheltenham last Whitsuntide Tuesday.'

At first light on Monday morning, 6 July, police activity at the murder scene was resumed. Deputy Chief Constable Hill found that 6yds from the entrance to the stableman's house, a trail of blood led across the cobbled yard for a distance of 12yds, ending at the spot where the body had lain the evening before. There were many footprints in the ash-strewn surface, but a lot of people had been present there only hours earlier. Near a large pool of the victim's congealed blood was a button matching those of the accused's shirt. A bloodstained collar and tie were found discarded in the brewhouse. There was no evidence in the cottage of disorder or of a struggle having taken place there.

A very dishevelled Bert Checketts was brought up before Alderman W.R. Selleck JP at Stourbridge Police Court, his hands still bloodstained, and now with a fresh abrasion visible on the bridge of his nose. Beneath his coat it could be seen that his shirt also was stained with blood. He made no reply when the Magistrate's Clerk, Mr W.W. King, read out the charge, accusing him of, 'feloniously, wilfully, and with malice aforethought, murdering Alice Mary Rowley.'

Deputy Chief Constable Hill told the magistrate:

In consequence of receiving a message from Inspector Halford last night, I accompanied him to Hickman's brickyard, where I saw the dead body of Alice Rowley lying on her back. She had a terrible wound in her throat. I ordered the removal of the body to the mortuary, then, I accompanied Inspector Halford to Lye Police Station where the prisoner was detained. I brought him to the police station here at Stourbridge, and after conversing with Dr Darby, who had examined the victim's body, I cautioned Checketts, and charged him with murdering Alice Rowley that evening by cutting her throat with a razor. He said, 'I am innocent', and went on to make a statement which I took down. I now ask for a remand in custody here until Wednesday to enable me to make further enquiries.

'You want to remand him to the cells here?' asked Mr King.

'Yes, sir.' replied the officer. The clerk then turned to Checketts and asked, 'Have you any cause to show why you should not be remanded until Wednesday?' to which the prisoner replied, 'Well, no sir.' Alderman Selleck then confirmed that the remand had been made for the next Wednesday at 4 p.m.

A considerable crowd of spectators assembled in the vicinity of the court later the same Monday afternoon to await the opening of the inquest, which was delayed for one hour to allow for the completion of the post-mortem examination. At 5 p.m., the proceedings were begun by the coroner, Mr F.P. Evers, who wore his wig and gown for the occasion. Mr Geoffrey Ince, deputy coroner, assisted throughout the three hour hearing. Lye solicitor, Mr W. Stanley Mobberley, was appointed to represent the accused, who remained in the police cells until after the verdict was reached.

After swearing in the foreman, Mr Frederick Biggs, and six fellow jurors, Mr Evers told them that whilst it was a very serious case, it was not one which he thought need cause them a very great amount of trouble, or need take a great deal of their time. He told them:

Shortly you will proceed to the mortuary to view the body of Alice Rowley, terribly injured, with frightful wounds in the throat and back of the neck, along with horrendous slashes around the breasts, abdomen, legs and shoulders. I have no doubt that you will see it would be quite impossible that these awful injuries could have been self-inflicted. That is a thing which you will mark when you see the body. There is nothing more now I think I need tell you, except that when you come to hear the evidence later, grave suspicion will fall upon a certain individual in connection with the case. You must bear in mind that whatever evidence there is against him, and whatever might be the nature of any defence put before some other court, the question of the man's state of mind does not concern yourselves. As a coroner's jury, you have to determine the cause of death. If the man who it was suggested as having inflicted the injuries was proved to be insane, that was a matter which would come before another court, and has nothing to do with what may transpire here. That is quite outside the jurisdiction of a coroner's court.

The jury then adjourned to view Miss Rowley's body.

Mrs Ellen Checketts, mother of the victim, was the first witness to be called as the court later sat to resume the inquiry. She was led to the witness box by a lady friend, where, being greatly distressed, she was provided with a chair. In a barely audible voice, she said she was the wife of James Checketts and resided at No. 132 Stourbridge Road, Lye. Her daughter, Alice, and stepson, Bert, also lived there too. Alice was twenty-two years of age on 11 November last. She was a single woman and worked in Messrs Hickman's brickyard, where their home was situated. At 9 p.m. on Sunday night, Mrs Checketts was in the Rose and Crown public house, when her daughter came to see her.

*Coroner:* 'What did she say to you?'
*Mrs Checketts:* 'She asked me to come across home.'
*Coroner:* 'Why?'
*Mrs Checketts:* 'She didn't say why.'
*Coroner:* 'Did she appear to be frightened or upset at all?'
*Mrs Checketts:* 'No.'
*Coroner:* 'When you went across home, who was in the house besides you and your daughter?'
*Mrs Checketts:* 'Bert, Bert Checketts.'
*Coroner:* 'Yes, what did your daughter say to you then?'
*Mrs Checketts:* 'She didn't say anything then. Bert came out of the house and up the yard. Then he walked out of the entrance gates and off towards Lye Cross.'
*Coroner:* 'Did she want you to fetch Bert away?'
*Mrs Checketts:* 'She didn't say.'
*Coroner:* 'What did Bert say when you were there?'
*Mrs Checketts:* 'He didn't say anything, but went right out of the house and up the yard with me.'
*Coroner:* 'Did your daughter seem to be satisfied when you took him away?'
*Mrs Checketts:* 'Yes. She didn't say anything then. She did not make a bit of a murmur then.'
*Coroner:* 'Had there been a quarrel?'
*Mrs Checketts:* 'That night?'
*Coroner:* 'At any time?'

*High Street, Lye. (Courtesy of Pat Dunn)*

*Mrs Checketts:* 'Not to my mind, though they have had a bother, but of course he has been quiet.'

*Coroner:* 'What was the bother about?'

*Mrs Checketts:* 'He has been ever so funny.'

*Coroner:* 'So did he quarrel with your daughter?'

*Mrs Checketts:* 'Not for me to hear him.'

Just then, the poor woman fainted, and was given a glass of cold water. When recovered, she continued to answer the coroner's questions as best she could.

*Coroner:* 'You say Bert had been ever so funny with your daughter?'

*Mrs Checketts:* 'Yes, but this was not lately.'

*Coroner:* 'He came out of the house, you say, and went up towards Lye Cross?'

*Mrs Checketts:* 'Yes. I did not see him afterwards.'

*Coroner:* 'He did not say anything, and you returned to the Rose and Crown?'

*Mrs Checketts:* 'Yes.'

*Coroner:* 'And did you next hear a row?'

*Mrs Checketts:* 'I don't know anything. I cannot remember anything else until they told me this morning.'

*Coroner:* 'They told you this morning that your daughter was dead?'

*Mrs Checketts:* 'Yes sir.'

Inspector Halford was invited to produce the bloodstained collar and tie, found by Deputy Chief Constable Hill in the brewhouse at the stableman's cottage, which was shown to Mrs Checketts. Without hesitation, she identified them as belonging to Bert Checketts.

Mr Mobberley said that the only point he wanted to mention was the statement of Mrs Checketts that her stepson was sometimes very funny. The coroner again asked the witness, 'When you went to the house, was Bert Checketts inside or outside?' She replied, 'He was in the house.' The coroner then said, 'I want to press you a little about this. Didn't you think it was rather unusual for your daughter to come and fetch you?'

'I hardly knew what to make of her fetching me', answered Mrs Checketts.

'And did she say anything to you on the way?' asked Mr Evers.

'No.' replied Mrs Checketts, that being her evidence completed.

Now her husband, James Checketts, was brought to the witness-box. He said that until about two and a half years previous, he was employed at Messrs Hickman's as a horse driver. The body he had seen in the mortuary was that of his step-daughter, Alice Mary Rowley. Checketts was first asked of the relationships between his son and his step daughter.

*Coroner:* 'What have been the feelings between one another?'

*Mr Checketts:* 'I cannot tell you exactly what their feelings have been, but I think he wanted to fall in love with her.'

*Coroner:* 'You think he did?'

*Mr Checketts:* 'I think he did, but I don't know for certain. I believe myself that he did.'

*Coroner:* 'She did not respond to his advances?'

*Mr Checketts:* 'No.'

*Coroner:* 'Do you know where he usually keeps his razor?'

At this point, the supposed murder weapon was produced in court. It was heavily bloodstained and a piece of the sharpened edge was chipped from the top of the blade.

*Mr Checketts:* 'He used to keep it in a little drawer, within the chest of drawers in the kitchen.'

*Coroner:* 'Was it there this morning?'

*Mr Checketts:* 'No. The case was there, but the razor was not in it.'

*Coroner:* 'Is this, the razor produced, the one that belonged to your son?'

*Mr Checketts:* 'Yes, that is the razor.'

*Coroner:* 'Did this refusal of hers to respond to his advances lead to trouble at any time?'

*Mr Checketts:* 'No, I never heard them quarrel. I don't believe he spoke to her yesterday; I don't think they spoke to one another at all yesterday.'

*Coroner:* 'Have you ever known him to threaten her?'

*Mr Checketts:* 'No.'

The foreman, Mr Biggs, asked if Mr Checketts had any knowledge of his son being funny towards his step-sister. 'Yes,' replied the witness. 'He was a bit funny sometimes.'

*Coroner:* 'Ill-tempered?'

*Mr Checketts:* 'No.'

*Coroner:* 'In what way?'

*Mr Checketts:* 'He used dirty ways towards her. He used to soil her clothes.'

*Foreman:* 'Did he ever molest her in any other way?'

*Mr Checketts:* 'No, I don't think he molested her in any other way.'

*Coroner:* 'Did you send for a doctor to deal with this?'

*Mr Checketts:* 'Yes, we consulted Dr Darby about his ways last December.'

*Coroner:* 'Did Alice Rowley complain to you about his conduct?'

*Mr Checketts:* 'No.'

*Coroner:* 'Had she any sweetheart beside. Had she anybody else courting her?'

*Mr Checketts:* 'Not that I am aware of. I never saw her with a young man. I don't know whether she had one or not.'

*Coroner:* 'When did you last see your son before this happened?'

*Mr Checketts:* 'I saw him when he went to church, I think in the evening.'

*Coroner:* 'That was somewhere about half past six?'

*Mr Checketts:* 'Yes, somewhere about that.'

*Foreman:* 'When did you know your step-daughter was dead?'

*Mr Checketts:* 'She was dead before I came home.'

*Foreman:* 'What time did you get home?'

*Mr Checketts:* 'It would be about 9.30 p.m.'

*Foreman:* 'Where was she then?'

*Mr Checketts:* 'She was then dead, lying in the stableyard. It drove me wild.'

*Foreman:* 'And have you seen your son since?'

*Mr Checketts:* 'No.'

Robert Collins, in giving evidence, said that he was employed by Messrs Hickman's as a brick burner. At about 9.20 p.m. the previous night, he was working at the ash bank, when his attention was drawn by two short screams which came from the direction of the stables. In reply to the coroner, he said that he was working about 150yds from the stableyard when he heard the screams. He walked towards the stables, but stopped when he saw Bert Checketts coming from the opposite direction. With about 50yds distance between them, Bert Checketts spotted him and turned around, retracing his steps back towards the stables. Asked by the coroner if, at the distance separating them, he could see anything as to the condition of Checketts' shirt sleeves, he answered that they seemed dirty, but he could not make out what had soiled them. It looked almost black.

He returned to his work, when about ten minutes later, he heard another scream, but this, he believed, to be from Mrs Checketts. When he arrived on the scene in the stableyard, Bert Checketts was there, along with a number of other people. It was then that he realised that the dark staining to Checketts' shirt was blood.

*Coroner:* 'Did he speak to you first or did you speak to him?'

*Mr Collins:* 'it was Checketts who spoke first.'

*Coroner:* 'What did he say?'

*Mr Collins:* 'He said, "I have not done it." I didn't know what he was talking about.'

*Coroner:* 'At that time, had you seen the body?'

*Mr Collins:* 'No. That was when I was walking towards the crowd of onlookers.'

*Coroner:* 'Then you saw the body lying on the ground?'

*Mr Collins:* 'Yes sir.'

*Coroner:* 'Where was she lying?'

*Mr Collins:* 'Three or four yards from the corner of the stables.'

*Coroner:* 'Was she fully dressed?'

*Mr Collins:* 'I don't think she had a hat on.'

*Coroner:* 'What was the condition of her clothing?'

*Mr Collins:* 'It was all bloodstained.'

*Coroner:* 'Was there a large wound in the throat?'

*Mr Collins:* 'Yes, I noticed that large one in the throat.'

*Coroner:* 'Did you notice any other wounds?'

*Mr Collins:* 'No sir.'

*Coroner:* 'Was her clothing disarranged in any way?'

*Mr Collins:* 'No sir, not when I got there. It had been straightened and she was lying straight.'

*Coroner:* 'There is one thing I want to ask you. How long elapsed between the time when you heard the two screams first and the time when you saw Checketts coming towards you?'

*Mr Collins:* 'It would not be more than a minute or a minute and a half at the most.'

*Coroner:* 'What was done? Were the police sent for?'

*Mr Collins:* 'I believe so. I didn't wait to see. I went back to my work.'

The coroner then changed the subject slightly:

*Coroner:* 'Take you mind back to Saturday about 7.30 p.m. Were you in the brickyard?'

*Mr Collins:* 'Yes.'

*Coroner:* 'And did you see Bert Checketts and Miss Rowley there?'

*Mr Colliins:* 'Yes.'

*Coroner:* 'Was there a quarrel going on between them?'

*Mr Collins:* 'There were shouting at one another, yes, quarrelling.'

*Coroner:* 'About lending a sixpence, was it not?'

*Mr Collins:* 'Yes. He was trying to get sixpence out of her.'

The foreman asked if Mr Collins did not think that he ought to have taken steps to see that the police were communicated with when, as might have been thought, a murder had been committed. 'Did you make enquiries whether the police had been sent for?' asked the coroner, to which Mr Collins replied, 'No sir.'

Deputy Chief Constable Hill suggested that other people had come on the scene. 'Yes sir.' agreed Mr Collins. The coroner asked, 'When there was this row on Saturday night, you interfered, didn't you?'

'Yes.' replied Mr Collins, 'I told Checketts that if he didn't get out of the yard, I would chuck him out. This was after Miss Rowley had told me what was the matter.'

'Did she appear to be frightened of him?' enquired the coroner.

'Yes sir.' said Mr Collins, before being excused from the witness box.

Police Constable Gerald Dadge said that he arrived at Hickman's brickyard at 9.55 p.m. on Sunday night, in consequence of a message received from one of the workforce. A large crowd was gathering in the stableyard, all viewing the body of a woman, lying on her back in a pool of blood.

*Coroner:* 'Did you see Bert Checketts there?'

*Dadge:* 'Yes. He came running out of the house nearby.'

*Coroner:* 'What was his condition?'

*Dadge:* 'He was in his shirt sleeves and covered with blood.'

*Coroner:* 'You did not know him before then?'

*Dadge:* 'No sir.'

*Coroner:* 'You spoke to him?'

*Dadge:* 'Yes. I said to him; "What is this then?"'

*Coroner:* 'What did he say?'

*Dadge:* 'He replied, "I am innocent. I am innocent. She did it herself. I tried to take the razor from her and I managed to get it out of her hands." That is all he said.'

*Coroner:* 'Did you find the bloodstained razor which has been produced here?'

*Dadge:* 'Yes sir. It was lying near the stable about 11 yds away from the body.'

Now Dr H.C. Darby entered the witness box. Sensationally, in delivering his post-mortem examination report, he revealed the full horrific extent of the appalling injuries suffered by Alice Rowley on that fateful night. First, the coroner asked, 'Had the body been moved at all?' Dr Darby replied, 'It probably had not been moved after death. I think some of the wounds were inflicted in one position and possibly the body then turned over, hence the dirt encrusted face.' The coroner then invited the doctor to read the findings of the autopsy, which had been conducted in the presence of his assistant, Dr Honigsberger.

Speaking of the external examination, Dr Darby said:

There was a scratch on the left ear a quarter of an inch long, and two small scratches on the nose. The throat was cut by an incision extending from a line drawn from the left ear to an inch below the right ear. Almost all the structures down to the spinal column were severed. The trachea was severed in three places, through the middle of the thyroid, about the level of the crico-thyroid membrane, and through the trachea.

The skin incisions were extremely jagged, and six incisions led into a gaping wound on the left side of the neck.

The coroner asked what the significance of the jagged wounds was. Dr Darby explained, 'They could hardly have been produced with one slash. They imply resistance.' He then continued to describe the lengthy catalogue of injuries, saying:

There were two more superficial wounds behind the neck and the chin, one wound on the lower lip ½in long, and another below the lip of the same size. There was a small incised wound on the chin and two abrasions like scratches, on the nose. There was a circular contusion, ³/₈ inches in diameter, near the angle of the jaw on the left side, and two linear contusions near the left temple, each 1in long.

On the trunk was an incised wound 4½in long and horizontal, reaching from the upper part of the armpit to the upper part of the breastbone. The right breast had a wound along the inner and lower edges 7in long, opening to 1½in wide near the middle. On the outer edge of the breast was an incised wound 4½in long, at skin depth only. Transversely, just above the nipple, was a wound 4½in in length, joining with the outer wound. Between these two were a number of small abrasions. The left breast had five incised and lacerated wounds running in the direction of from below and upwards. These were mostly on the upper and inner sections of the breast.

Coroner: 'Could all these wounds have been caused by a razor?'

Dr Darby: 'Yes. They have probably been produced by a razor.'

Coroner: 'Had these wounds on the trunk identified with corresponding marks on the clothing?'

Dr Darby: 'The clothing had been removed before I saw the body at the mortuary earlier this morning. I endeavoured to compare the wounds on the body with cuts in the clothing, but it was very difficult to adjust the clothing to the body. This was due to the clothing being saturated with blood, and it had probably been forcibly removed from the body. It was hard to distinguish what damage was caused to the clothing in the attack or alternatively in the mortuary.'

Coroner: 'From your inspection of the body and the clothing, do you think these wounds were inflicted while she was clothed?'

Dr Darby: 'I know the wounds were inflicted whilst she was clothed because I saw her lying in the stableyard with her clothing on. At that time, I saw the gash on her breast through the chemise she was wearing. I also saw the incisions in the neck and many of the minor injuries at the same time.'

The coroner observed that it was unthinkable that all of these wounds were inflicted in such a short period of time, before urging the doctor to progress with his report. Continuing his description of the injuries, he said there was a small abrasion about 1in long, below the breast, shaped like three sides of a square. In the lower part of the abdomen there was an incision 3½in long on the left side. The upper part of this wound was very superficial, suggesting it had been inflicted in an upwards stroke. To the right side of the abdomen was an incision 6in long and evidently inflicted in the same manner.

Dealing with the limbs, he said that on the right upper arm was an incised wound over the shoulder, near to the acromio-clavicular joint, ½inch long. Another wound was on the outer side of the right arm. It was crescent-shaped, measuring 3in by 3¼in, being 1½in deep. On the inner side of the elbow joint was an incised wound 6½in long, but only skin deep. On the inner side of the forearm was a series of bruising varying from ¼ inches to ¾ inches in diameter.

A 7½in oblique wound was inflicted about one third of the way down on the right thigh, which was deeper at its inner extremity. On the inner side of the left thigh there were seven distinct incised wounds, somewhat radiating, but mostly lengthways and deeper at the lower ends. The back of the left leg bore an incision 6in long, extending from the gluteal fold inwardly and down the centre of the leg.

At the back of the head, one inch below the occipital protrudement and extending outwards to the left for 2½in, was an incised wound. Lower down, at the junction of the neck and trunk, over the seventh vertebra, was another incised wound of 5½in length, almost meeting with the wound in the front.

Astonishingly, the doctor had counted no less than forty separate wounds, with the possibility of there having been up to fifty thrusts being made with a razor. He found all the body's organs to be normal and healthy, and the woman had been well nourished.

*Coroner:* 'What was the actual cause of death?'

*Dr Darby:* 'Shock from hemorrhage.'

*Coroner:* 'From which wounds?'

*Dr Darby:* 'The neck injuries.'

*Coroner:* 'Have you formed any opinion as to whether the trunk and limb wounds were caused after death?'

*Dr Darby:* 'Some of them might have been.'

*Coroner:* 'The whole of these wounds could have been inflicted with the razor?'

*Dr Darby:* 'Yes sir.'

*Coroner:* 'Could the wounds that caused death, the neck wounds of which you speak, have been self-inflicted?'

*Dr Darby:* 'I think it not likely.'

*Coroner:* 'Could you say whether any of the injuries to the throat or neck appear to have been inflicted from behind?'

*Dr Darby:* 'I think those injuries on the front of the neck were inflicted from behind.'

Dr Darby said that in the presence of Deputy Chief Constable Hill, he examined Bert Checketts at Stourbridge police station in the early hours of the morning. On the inner side of the little finger of the right hand, there was a cut ⅞in long, and a scratch near the wrist ¼in long. On the inner side of the thumb was a cut ⅜in long.

On the outer side of the index finger on the left hand was another cut measuring ³⁄₈in. Over the end of the same finger was a cut ½in long. There was a bloodstain on the lining of the man's trousers. There were also other stains, which could only be decided by microscopic examination.

After also hearing Deputy Chief Constable Hill's account of Checketts arrest, the coroner said that all the evidence had now been produced. He did not think there was much he need say to the jury, because the case seemed a very clear one. No one appeared to have witnessed the crime being committed, but all the circumstances seemed to point in one direction. If they thought the evidence justified, they would not hesitate to find a verdict of wilful murder against this man. Soon after some screams were heard, Checketts was found with blood all over him and his razor was found on the ground in near proximity to the victim's body. It seemed there was very little doubt, but he would leave it to the jury, and if they thought the circumstances justified, they would not hesitate to bring a verdict in keeping with their duty.

At 7.50 p.m., the jury retired, the foreman, Mr Biggs, returning only four minutes later. He said they were quite satisfied that the poor woman met her death through the wounds inflicted by Bert Checketts, and therefore they returned a verdict of 'wilful murder' against the man.

Checketts was fetched from the police cells and placed barefoot in the prisoner's box. Mr Evers addressed him, 'Bert Checketts, the jury have found you guilty of the wilful murder of Alice Mary Rowley.' A gleam of amusement was seen to flicker across Checketts' face. He appeared to be poised to speak, but made no remark. Immediately afterwards, he was escorted back down the steps to the cells below.

The following day, Tuesday 7 July, a reporter from the *Worcestershire County Express* interviewed the prisoner's father, Mr James Checketts. The representative was told that, whilst temperate in habits, his son used to enjoy a half pint on occasions, 'But I have never known him drunk.' added Mr Checketts. The reporter suggested that Bert Checketts was fond of his step-sister, Mr Checketts replying:

> Oh yes, but she didn't want him. He used to have it he liked her, but she wouldn't have anything to do with him. I begged him to forget her and say nothing more to her, and let her find a young man if she wanted one. They never quarreled as I know to. She would not talk to him. She was a steady wench, and never went away much, but always wanted to be at work. It's a funny affair, they lived in the same house, but never said a lot to one another. We all had our evening meal together on Sunday and were very comfortable together.

A neighbour, who had known the accused all his life, said, 'I didn't think that he could hurt a worm. He was what you would call 'a simple hard one', although there seemed to be no harm in him.' It was also revealed by the press that, prior to the killing, Checketts had predicted to his fellow horse-racing fraternity that, 'Dragon will win at Nottingham on Monday', the horse actually winning at good odds!

On Wednesday, at the appointed time, 4 p.m., Checketts was again brought before Alderman W.R. Selleck JP, escorted into the makeshift courtroom by Constables Lovejoy and Hodges. About three dozen men were assembled in small groups outside the police station, but no members of the public were admitted into the charge room, where the proceedings took place. The only other persons present were the Deputy Chief Constable, solicitor Mr Mobberley, magistrates clerk Mr Major Pardoe, Inspector Halford and four press reporters.

Mr Pardoe read the charge: 'Bert Checketts, you are charged that on 5 July 1925, you did feloniously, wilfully and with malice aforethought, kill and murder one Alice Rowley.' The prisoner made no reply.

The Deputy Chief Constable, Mr Hill, explained that at the inquest held the previous day, the jury had returned a verdict of 'wilful murder' against the prisoner. 'And now sir,' Mr Hill told the magistrate, 'I ask that you remand him in custody until Friday.' Alderman Selleck spoke to Checketts, 'Have you anything to say why you should not be remanded until Friday?'

'Not to that, sir', replied Checketts.

'Then you are remanded until Friday', concluded Alderman Selleck. The accused, quickly stepping, then left the room, the hearing altogether lasting just five minutes.

At 3.35 p.m. on Thursday 9 July, a wreath-covered patent black hearse, followed by a family coach, pulled out of Hickman's brickyard to convey the mortal remains of Alice Rowley to their last resting place. As a mark of esteem, the brickworks had closed at 11.30 a.m. for the rest of the day. Several hundred spectators, some of whom had gathered an hour before, lined the road opposite the entrance gates and nearby stables where the poor woman had met her untimely death.

The cortège emerged into Stourbridge Road, followed by many colleagues from the brickyard, and proceeded to Lye Cross, before turning into Pedmore Road, where the girls employed by Messrs Ludlow Bros left their work for a short time to pay their last respects. At the gates to Lye and Wollescote Cemetery, a vast throng in excess of 3,000 people awaited the arrival of the hearse, behind which seven close workmates followed on foot. Quite 2,000 more lined the long drive leading to the cemetery chapel where a full congregation heard the Revd A.G. Lewis, vicar of St Mark's, Stambermill, conduct the burial service.

Missing from the bereaved was the deceased's mother, who was too ill to attend. However, her step-father sat with her four elder sisters; Mrs E. Wilkinson, Mrs T. Dawes, Mrs J. Taylor and Mrs A. Stafford, who, all overcome with grief, wept bitterly throughout. Other family members included step-brothers James, Robert and John Checketts; cousin Louisa and aunts Eliza and Louisa. Close friend, Mrs Cissie Wootton sat nearby.

Hickman's foreman, Mr A. Davies, was joined by fellow workers; Alice Hart, Ann Worton, Ellen Davies, Susan Palmer, Martha Richards, Lily Thompson, Harry Hall, William Boaler, William Brooks, Bert Davies, James Raybould and several others.

*Lye brickyard workers. (Courtesy of Pat Dunn)*

Following the service, amidst much solemnity, the coffin was carried to the graveside, the bearers being; E. Wilkinson, T. Dawes, J. Taylor, J. Rowley, B. Round and J.T. Pearson, all male relatives of the deceased. The assembled crowd, made up of Stourbridge residents, and those of the surrounding districts of Old Hill, Brierley Hill, Cradley, Cradley Heath and Quarry Bank, listened in dignified silence as the Revd Lewis read the committal lines, as the coffin was lowered into the ground by Mr Sidney F. Davies and staff, funeral directors of nearby Pedmore Road.

The whole proceedings were policed by Sergeant Houghton, assisted by three constables and passed off without any untoward incident, the many thousands present exhibiting the most orderly of conduct.

The following day, at 11.30 a.m., the case against Bert Checketts was resumed at Stourbridge Police Court. Considerable public interest was manifested, with a large crowd gathering outside the police station buildings, seventy of whom gained admittance to the courtroom, filling to capacity all of the public accommodation.

The Mayor of Stourbridge, Mr Randle L. Mathews JP, sat as Chairman of the Magistrates, joined by fellow Justices of the Peace; Lieutenant Colonel A.H. Moody CBE, Alderman Felix P. Fellows, Mr H.E. Palfrey CC, Mr J.T. Worton CC, Mr Claude S. Trow and Mr A.H. Gordon. Lye solicitor, Mr W. Stanley Mobberley, again represented the interests of the accused, whilst Mr B.G. Saywell from London appeared for the Office of the Public Prosecutor. Shortly before arriving at the court, Mr Saywell had

*Lye and Wollescote Cemetery, where Alice Mary Rowley rests in peace. (Author's collection)*

made an inspection of the site of the alleged murder, accompanied by Deputy Chief Constable Hill. Also present was coroner Mr F.P. Evers, upon whose warrant the prisoner already stood committed upon the capital charge.

Checketts was brought up the steps from the cells and led to a chair provided in the dock. It was going to be a lengthy hearing. No trace of emotion was discernible on his face, as he sat quietly, dressed in a dark suit with neither collar nor tie.

Following Mr Saywell's outlining of the case, Mr H.E. Folkes, surveyor, of Stourbridge, was called to produce a ground plan he had made of No. 132 Stourbridge Road, Lye, and the surrounding brickyard. He had indicated on the plan various positions and their distances apart. At one spot, in front of the stables, he had found the ground darkly stained over an area of 4ft-sq., the grotesque aftermath of the slaying of the tragic Alice Rowley. Afterwards, photographer Mr Charles Gerard Mason, handed to the magistrates two prints showing the cottage and stableyard, taken on the instructions of the Deputy Chief Constable.

The first eyewitness to give evidence, Millie Pardoe, wife of Mr Percy Pardoe, told of walking across the fields from Stourbridge railway junction, but hearing no screams from the nearby brickyard. When stopped by Bert Checketts at the entrance gates, and shown the body of Alice Rowley, although she knew the victim well, she failed to recognise her, commenting, 'She looked a biggish woman, about fifty years old I would say.'

Mrs Ellen Checketts, who only the day before had been too overcome with grief to attend her daughter's funeral, was next shown to the witness stand. Evidently still in a very distressed state, dressed in black, she had to be helped to the box by her sister, where she was accommodated in a comfortable chair. From time to time, her sister soothed her sympathetically, and gave her the occasional sip from a glass of water.

Whilst answering questions put to her by Mr Mobberley, she was shown Bert Checketts' bloodstained collar and tie and asked to identify them, causing her to sob pitifully. It was observed that the prisoner remained quite unmoved at his step-mother's distress, his cold demeanour unbroken. After a one-hour adjournment for lunch, Checketts entered the courtroom before the spectators returned to their seats in the public gallery. For a few moments, he took a keen interest in watching those who came in, before settling down in his chair and resuming his former attitude.

For the next two hours, the court heard detailed evidence from Dr Darby, repeating the most gruesome results of his post-mortem examination. Mr Mobberley posed the question, 'Assuming that some person had done all this, would you regard that person as mentally balanced?'

'I am afraid I must ask you what you mean by mental balance', replied the doctor.

'Would you regard such a person as possessing the workings of a disordered mind? If any person had carried out what you found on this body, would you regard that person as having a properly balanced mind?' clarified the solicitor. In answer, Dr Darby said, 'The number and character of the injuries would suggest to me that whoever committed them was not, at that time, in the normal state of mind.'

The doctor told of examining Checketts on 3 December, the previous year, at the request of the accused's father. On that occasion, he reproved him about his conduct towards his step-sister. He appeared to understand what was said to him and promised he would not do it again.

Mr Mobberley then asked, 'From your knowledge of the prisoner, would you say that he was not normal?' In reply, the doctor stated:

I formed the opinion that this man was not an idiot or a person of insane memory from birth, and in my opinion, neither was he an imbecile, which is a stage higher than an idiot, and is a person having a certain amount of intelligence. I think he is a stage higher than that because he has, in my opinion, some knowledge of sense of what is right and wrong.

Later in the afternoon, Mr James Checketts told of his son's strange behaviour in following his step-sister about town, explaining, 'When she went out, he would walk after her and follow her some distance behind. He never walked with her. She used to come home and tell us that he had been following her, and I used to grumble to him about this.'

Towards the end of the hearing, Mr Saywell submitted for the prosecution that upon the evidence given, a presumption of guilt had been raised, and he therefore asked the magistrates to commit the accused to take his trial at the assizes. Checketts was then formally charged with wilful murder, but gave no reply.

Mr Mobberley submitted that by his cross-examination, he had indicated a line of defence sufficient to warrant the Bench in granting a certificate under the Poor Prisoners Defence Act 1903. The court granted Mr Mobberley a fee of £3 3s for the said certificate, then committed Checketts to take his trial at the next Worcestershire Assizes. The proceedings lasted until 6.20 p.m. During the whole of this time, the accused sat with his arms folded, staring for the most part straight in front of himself.

The trial was held on Friday 23 October 1925 before Judge Mr Justice Roche. The case for the prosecution was presented by Mr G.K. Rose, and for the defence by Mr Earengay, on the instructions of the accused's solicitor, Mr Mobberley.

The jurors, chiefly from the districts of Blackheath and Halesowen, were named as; Herbert Eldred Lewis (foreman), David Brittain, Arthur Rowley, Arthur Ernest Kelly, George Frederick Spruce, George Brinton, Edwin Adams, Thomas Henry Browning, William Griffiths, Edwin Sawyer, James Henry Stone and Frank West.

Bert Checketts was brought up to the dock escorted by two prison warders. He walked steadily, with his hands clasped behind his back. When read the charge, without hesitation he replied, 'Not guilty sir', although his voice was curiously thick and strangled. During the hearing, he showed only the slightest interest in the case being made against him, instead spending much of the time leaning back in his chair, his eyes fixed on the ceiling above.

At one sensational point in the proceedings, Mr Earengay was making an effort to pose a question dealing with the sexual aspect of the evidence in such a way as to be least offensive to the women who were present in the courtroom, when the judge stopped him and declared, 'This detail, to my mind, is essential to the understanding of the case, and the jury must have it clearly. The remedy of the people who are excited by curiosity is not to be here. If they choose to come to a case like this it cannot be helped.'

Rather emphatically, the judge in examination of Dr Hamblin Smith, medical officer of Winson Green Prison, Birmingham, cogently put it to him, 'Is it a fact that in some men there survives what may be called 'animal passion', the attacking of the female in the excitement of sexual feeling?'

'Certainly my Lord.' replied the doctor.

'Some animals do actually kill the female during or after the act, do they not?' suggested the judge. The doctor readily agreed. Then, to clinch the issue, the judge put it to Dr Hamblin Smith, 'Assuming that this man did what was done to this woman that evening, is that, in your opinion, a possible or probable explanation of what happened?'

'Yes my Lord; I think it is certainly possible, and I go further to say I think it is probable.' came the doctor's reply.

Mr Earengay, in his speech for the defence, said that the case had been distasteful to all connected with it. It was a sordid case. He wanted to impress on the jury that it was obviously useless to attempt to ask Checketts to make any statement. His case was that the prisoner's explanation, 'I am innocent, I did not do it', represented his view of what actually happened. He did not ask the jury to accept it as a true explanation, but if the jury were satisfied that Checketts really believed the girl had killed herself, he asked them to say that the prisoner was insane. He submitted that the accused was under par, a child in capacity and understanding, a child who never grew up, and whose mind was clearly diseased.

In summing up the case, the judge addressed the jury, saying:

> I suppose that the first thought in your minds was sympathy with the unhappy woman who was killed in the brickyard on that terrible Sunday evening last July. However, as the trial has progressed, I expect that your sympathy has shifted to the man in the dock. Do not think, when I direct you in a sense adverse to the contention of the defence, that I am unaffected by such sympathy, or that I am directing you in the law out of hardness of heart. You can rest assured I do it only out of my sense of duty. I am going to tell you my judgement according to the law, and I say frankly there are insufficient reasons for finding a verdict of 'guilty but insane' as suggested by the defence.

The jury retired at 1.45 p.m. At 2.30 p.m., the foreman announced that a 'guilty' verdict had been reached. Mr Justice Roche placed the black cap upon his head and told the prisoner:

> The sentence of this court is that you be taken to a place of lawful execution, to be there hanged by the neck until you are dead, and that your body shall be buried in the confines of the prison in which you last were, and may God have mercy on your soul.

A subdued voice in the body of the court added a terse 'Amen'. There then followed a tense silence. Bert Checketts stood to attention in the dock between two escorts. He had listened to the pronouncement without the slightest sign of emotion. He was entirely unmoved and stared at the judge vacantly, before glancing around at the awed witnesses to the event. The tension was only broken when an official touched the condemned man on the arm, and signalled him to leave the dock and descend the steps to the cells. Checketts stepped firmly down the stairs and out of view. The judge then rose, bowed to the jury, and also left.

The crowd occupying the public gallery, who, after the adjournment of the court, had rushed back to their seats like rowdy cinema goers, and had laughed and joked while awaiting the return of the judge and jury, left the courtroom silently, with many of the women shedding tears.

The following week, a petition was submitted to the Home Secretary, prepared by Messrs W.S. Mobberley & Son on behalf of James and Ellen Checketts, urging him to,

'Call for a report upon the prisoner's mental condition, and also peruse the official notes of the judge's summing up.'

In the meantime, the parents received a letter from their undaunted son stating:

> Just a few lines hoping that you are alright and happy at home, as it leaves me right up to the time of writing this letter. I went up to London to hear the appeal, but it was dismissed. I still think that I have a chance of being reprieved of the crime they say I've done. I daresay you will be coming to see me, and I shall be very pleased to see you. Remember me to all my friends. Kisses for Bess and all.

The prisoner's confidence was validated when Messrs Mobberley were communicated with by the Home Office on 20 November with the following message:

> Gentlemen, with reference to your letters of 29 October and 12 November, on behalf of Bert Checketts, who was recently convicted of murder and sentenced to death. I am directed by the Secretary of State to acquaint you that he has felt warranted, under all the circumstances, in advising His Majesty to respite the Capital sentence with a view to its commutation to Penal Servitude for life. I am your obedient servant, E. Blackwell.

Checketts parents were assured by the Governor of Winson Green Prison that their son would be well cared for when removed to Parkhurst or Maidstone, which would probably be done the following week.

# 7

# 'I'VE DONE SALLY IN'

## *West Bromwich, 1926*

It is often said that 'lightening never strikes in the same place twice'. You may find that the residents of the Hill Top district of West Bromwich would disagree, especially when the Hilly-Piece and Rydding Square are brought to mind. Let me take you back to Monday 20 September 1926, a little under twenty-six years after the dreadful murder of local youngster Matilda Coleyshaw (*see* Chapter One). At five minutes past midnight, twenty-four-year-old Joseph Leatherland was lying stretched

*Rydding Square, West Bromwich, as it is today. (Author's collection)*

out on the sofa at No. 60 Rydding Square, waiting for the return of his elder brother, Edward, aged twenty-eight, a labourer at W.H. Keys Ltd, Hall End Oilworks, Church Lane, West Bromwich.

Edward Leatherland entered the house and gave his brother a tap on the shoulder asking 'Joe, where's mother and father?' Joseph replied, 'In bed where they ought to be.' At that, Edward opened the door to the stairs and shouted 'Mother, I've done Sally in.' Joseph sprung from the sofa and closed the stairs door. He asked, 'You haven't really done Sally in, have you?' His brother repeated what he had said and pulled back his jacket to reveal a heavily bloodstained shirt. It was then noticed that his hands were also covered with blood. 'Where have you done it, Ted?', asked a shocked Joseph.

'You know where the Hilly-piece is, Joe, the place where they loose horses?'

'Yes, I know where it is,' replied Joseph, adding 'come and take me to where you have done Sally in.'

He knew well that by 'Sally', his brother meant near neighbour Sarah Brookes, a thirty-eight-year-old war widow and mother of three children; Horace, sixteen, Kathleen, twelve, and Ernest, aged ten. Her late husband, Leonard, was killed in France in 1916 whilst serving in the Oxford and Buckinghamshire Light Infantry. She had been intimate with Edward Leatherland for three months, frequently inviting him into her home, No. 38 Rydding Square, where they had enjoyed clandestine moments of passion.

The two brothers left Rydding Square, but before they reached the top of Crookhay Lane (their intended route to the Hilly-Piece), Joseph changed his mind and instead persuaded Edward to continue along Witton lane and towards Hill Top police station. On patrol in Rydding Square was Police Constable Bird, who, curious of the brothers hurried pace, decided to follow. At 12.20 a.m., Edward Leatherland entered the station lobby where Constable John Pinxton was on desk duty. He was somewhat startled when Leatherland blurted out 'Put the handcuffs on me, Mr Pinxton. I have done a murder.' Constable Pinxton sat the anguished young man and his brother down. On his return, Constable Bird was sent to summon colleague Constable Cartwright. After being cautioned, Leatherland gave the following statement;

> The woman whom I have been knocking about with, I have done her in. I have done
> it with a brick and a bottle and I have strangled her. You will find her against the wall
> down Crookhay Lane. I took a razor with me, but she knocked it out of my hand.
> I did it half an hour ago.

Leatherland was then taken into custody and the officer-in-charge, Sergeant Benton, sent for. In consequence of what he had heard, Sergeant Benton walked down Crookhay Lane to the Hilly-Piece. About 7ft into the field, Sarah Brookes' body lay face up, her shattered head pointing towards the heavily bloodstained wall. Her arms were thrown back and her skin was still warm to the touch. Dr Thomas Heywood

*The entrance to the former Hill Top police station and adjoining Sergeant's House. It is now the library and community centre. (Author's collection)*

Sansome was called to the scene from his residence, 'The Poplars', at Hill Top. He pronounced that life was extinct.

As dawn broke over the Hilly-Piece, the full horror of the aftermath could clearly be seen. The victim's face and head were hideously battered and two false teeth attached to a small dental plate lay nearby, as did the woman's handbag. All around was found broken glass and a bloodied lump of furnace cinder with several strands of hair stuck to it. Two halves of a razor case could be seen, one with a clean razor protruding from it.

Following the removal of the body to the mortuary, Sergeant Benton returned to Hill Top police station and formerly charged Leatherland with the murder of Sarah Brookes. In reply to the charge, Leatherland said, 'That's right, I done Sarah Brookes in. I used two beer bottles, hit her on the forehead and strangled her. She gave me venereal disease. I think life is not worth living.'

Later that same Monday morning, Leatherland appeared at the law courts, Lombard Street West, in West Bromwich town centre, before Justices of the Peace Alderman Joseph Edward Cox, Mrs F.K. Parish, Frederick Scarfe and Mr T. Foley Bache. The large crowd that jostled in the court precincts for a view of the accused were disappointed when he was led from the prison van through a side door. At 5ft 8in tall, he exhibited a dishevelled appearance as he stood in the dock, still wearing the mud-spattered navy-blue suit in which he was arrested. Mr J.S. Sharpe was engaged to represent the prisoner, the very same solicitor who spoke for Matilda

Coleyshaw's murderer, Joseph Lowe, over a quarter of a century before. Clerk to the Magistrates, Mr W.J. Phair, read out the charge followed by Chief Superintendent Tucker acquainting the court with the known facts before applying for a remand in custody so that the case could be prepared and laid before the Director of Public Prosecutions. With Mr Sharpe making no objection, the prisoner was remanded until the following Monday. As he left the dock, several women sitting at the back of the public gallery shouted 'Cheerio, Teddy', which he acknowledged with a smile.

At his own request, Leatherland attended the inquest upon the body of Sarah Brookes, which opened the following day, Tuesday 21 September, at the same law courts. Officiating before a jury, the coroner, Mr Lyon Clark, called only one witness, Mr Richard Henry Mole, a brother of the deceased who gave evidence of identification. Mr Clark later adjourned the inquest until Friday 1 October explaining that as Dr Sansome's medical examination of the deceased was still ongoing, it would be in the interests of the public not to continue with the matter until the full medical evidence was available.

Rydding Square was reportedly packed with 'a crowd of fully 300 mourners, most of them women', when the funeral cortège assembled in the afternoon of Monday 27 September to convey the mortal remains of Sarah Brookes to West Bromwich Cemetery. Spectators assembled at every vantage point, with many leaning from upstairs windows as the procession moved on, headed by the victim's three orphaned children. One witness to be observed by the press was 'the father of the man now in custody'.

*West Bromwich cemetery, showing the now demolished chapel. (Author's collection)*

The departure of the hearse signalled a hurried move of the crowd along Witton Lane and then up Heath Lane, towards the main entrance of the cemetery. There was much disappointment when it was realised that the police had closed the wrought iron gates, where an equally large group had earlier assembled. Despite the police precautions, numerous people had gathered within the burial ground up to two hours before their arrival. In a simple ceremony conducted by Mr A.J. Bowles, the body was interred in the re-opened family grave, which was afterwards quickly filled in to avoid as much 'sight seeing' as possible. The police made a 20ft privacy zone around the plot.

The two orphan boys bore the ordeal fairly well, but their sister, being much distressed, made for a pitiful sight. Messrs William Smalley of Hill Top carried out the funeral arrangements throughout. Of the five wreaths and a few bunches of flowers placed over the grave, one poignant message simply ended, 'From the neighbours of Rydding Square'.

Earlier that day, Leatherland was in court again on another remand appearance before the Stipendiary Magistrate. This time, he presented a much smarter picture, having been provided with a clean change of clothing. He must have enjoyed the reputation of being something of a 'ladies man' for, as previously when last in court, a group of female admirers broke into a chorus of 'Good morning, Teddy ', as he waved and left the dock.

On Friday 1 October, as previously arranged, the coroner, Mr Lyon Clark, resumed the inquest upon the death of Sarah Brookes, on which occasion Dr Sansome was able to give a more accurate, if somewhat gruesome report of his post-mortem findings. He found that there were numerous wounds to the hands consistent with having put up a defence. The skull had received fractures in several places and the nose and front teeth were broken. Her lips were quite bruised. An open wound on her right check measured 1in by 1½in. Another on the forehead was 3½in by 2½in. There were bruises on both arms above the elbows, which were consistent with thumb pressure other than those of the victim. The cause of death was shock brought about by the severity of the injuries. Certain organs were removed and sent to Professor Charles H. Wilson at the pathology department of Birmingham University. He subjected them to examination and as a result was of the opinion that they belonged to someone who suffered from chronic venereal disease. It was at that point in his evidence that Dr Sansome divulged that Leatherland had consulted him on Thursday 16 September, three days prior to the murder, on which occasion the doctor diagnosed him as being infected with the same sexually transmitted condition.

The coroner, in summing-up, advised the jury to disregard any rumours they had heard about the district or what was printed in the local newspapers, but to confine themselves strictly to the evidence put before them at that inquiry. The evidence in truth commenced when Edward Leatherland consulted Dr Sansome on the Thursday. From what they had been told, they would have to answer the following questions. 'They would have to say what was the medical cause of death, and they should have no difficulty with that. They would have to decide whether death resulted as a consequence of the injuries received, and they should have no difficulty with that also.'

The next questions were, 'How was each injury caused and by what instrument or weapon? By whom the injuries were caused?' and 'Did Edward Leatherland receive great and considerable provocation?' The coroner urged that they had to consider whether Leatherland was suffering under a great sense of wrong which had been done him by Sarah Brookes. He pointed out though that they must bear in mind that he knew of his condition on the Thursday previous when Dr Sansome examined him, and what took place was after an interval of three full days. Was it possible for Leatherland to be smarting under this wrong for three days and then murdered her in a sudden explosion of passion, for if he had done it when totally unbalanced of mind and not master of himself, the verdict would be one of manslaughter. Yet in the total absence of that, and he did it whilst quite himself, then their verdict would be one of murder. He asked the jury to assume that Leatherland had this complaint, and to assume that it was transmitted from Sarah Brookes, but did sufficient time elapse between the Thursday and Sunday for the passion to subside. The jury then retired to consider their verdict.

In one hour, the jury returned to court and presented their findings to the coroner. Reading from a paper, he declared that the jury had agreed that the medical cause of death was as stated by the doctor. That death followed as a consequence of the injuries which had been caused by a piece of cinder and two bottles and that the injuries had been inflicted by Edward Leatherland wielding the said weapons, whilst under great and considerable provocation. As to the question whether sufficient time had elapsed for his passion to subside and for reason to prevail, the jury replied in the affirmative, the effect of which was a verdict of murder.

The formal charge of Capital Murder was put to Edward Leatherland on Monday 4 October, when he appeared before Mr A. Vaughan JP and Sir Harris Spencer, at West Bromwich Law Court. Mr W.A. Saywell, acting for the Director of Public Prosecutions placed the facts of the case before the magistrates and heard the various witnesses repeat the evidence they had earlier given at the inquest. Defending solicitor, Mr J.S. Sharpe, requested that his client be seated throughout the hearing and the magistrates obliged. He sat between two prison warders from Winson Green, presenting a quiet and composed manner and occasionally turning to smile at his parents who sat amongst other relatives in the courtroom.

In answer to the charge, Mr Sharpe spoke on Leatherland's behalf saying, 'The accused formally pleads not guilty, does not wish to call any witnesses today and reserves his defence.' Clerk to the magistrates, Mr W.J. Phair, asked Leatherland, 'Is that what you want to say?' He replied, 'Yes, Sir.' When the chairman committed him for trial at Staffordshire Winter Assizes, he added, 'Thank you, Sir.' As he was led from the dock, he waved his hand to several female admirers in the public gallery, who wished him, 'Good afternoon, Ted.' Someone was heard to shout, 'Don't forget, Ted', his response being, 'I'll do my best.'

Edward Leatherland seemed to be less composed than at his earlier court appearances when his trial was opened by Mr Justice Rigby Swift KC, at Stafford on Monday 15 November 1926. In a steady voice he pleaded 'Not guilty' when the charge was put to him that on Sunday 19 September last, at Hill Top, West Bromwich, he did wilfully murder Mrs Sarah Brookes. Members of her family sat amongst those of the accused, alongside others from West Bromwich in a packed public gallery. Mr W.S. Morrison prosecuted for the Crown, whilst Leatherland's defence was led by Mr H.A. Tucker, on the instructions of Messrs Sharpe and Millichip, solicitors.

The judge began with a summary of events that day, a very special day in the Leatherland household, with Mrs Leatherland celebrating her fiftieth year. A birthday party was thrown at No. 60 Rydding Square attended by family and close neighbours including Sarah Brookes. Emily Leatherland, sister of the accused, had returned to the family home earlier in the day to help arrange the special occasion, taking the train from Manchester where she was employed in domestic service. At 7 p.m., with the celebrations over, Emily was escorted by her parents to Wednesbury Central railway station in Great Western Street, to catch the train back to Manchester. Joining them was her brother Edward, accompanied by Sarah Brookes, who both decided to board the train with Emily, saying their goodbyes at Wolverhampton station and then taking the return train back to Wednesbury.

*Wednesbury Central railway station, now demolished. (Courtesy of Terry Price)*

On the walk back to Hill Top, they stopped off at a public house, consuming four or five pints of ale between them, before leaving at closing time with a further two sealed bottles. At the top of Holloway Bank, they turned left into the Colliery Road to take a shortcut to Crookhay Lane over the Hilly-Piece.

However, only Edward Leatherland completed the journey back to Rydding Square, leaving again minutes later and walking directly to Hill Top police station where he volunteered a confession to a most ghastly murder. The accused had previously been a law-abiding citizen who served his country four years in the Army in France and Egypt.

The first witness to be called was Police Constable Bird, who explained that earlier in the evening, he had seen the Leatherland family members joined by Sarah Brookes crossing the tramlines in Holloway Bank whilst walking in the direction of Wednesbury. His next sighting of the accused was near to midnight, when Leatherland was seen hurrying home from the direction of Crookhay Lane, then leaving his home about five minutes later accompanied by his brother Joseph.

Then William James Haynes, a furnace hand, of No. 73 Witton Lane, took the stand to give his evidence. He told of entering the Hilly-Piece after first crossing the Tame Valley Canal at Ball's Hill Bridge on his return from a night out at Wednesbury. Shortly after 11 p.m., he noticed a couple walking in the direction of Crookhay Lane, but owing to the darkness could not make out who they were. Suddenly he heard a woman call out, 'Ted, don't go yet, stop a minute.' He then recognised the voice as that of Sarah Brookes. The man was walking some yards ahead and shouted back, 'I'm going home, I am.' This voice, he knew, belonged to Edward Leatherland.

Mrs Brookes was calling for Leatherland to turn back, protesting that she had sprained her ankle. Leatherland only repeated what he had earlier said. Mr Haynes walked in the same direction ahead of the pair, but stopped to rest when he reached Crookhay Lane, sitting on the boundary wall. Shortly before he moved on, he noticed that the couple were walking in close company again, Mrs Brookes with a pronounced limp. This time, he heard no conversation and it was the last sighting he had of them that night.

Joseph Leatherland recounted his brother's arrival home at 12.05 a.m. and subsequent confession to the slaying of Sarah Brookes. As the witness described how his brother said he had carried out the attack, Mrs Leatherland broke down and had to be led from court, her husband following shortly afterwards. Then, by the judge's direction, the bloodstained shirt worn that night was brought into court and exhibited to the jury. Later, in reply to Mr Morrison, Joseph Leatherland stated that his brother had never previously made any complaint to him about the deceased ever having given him any disease. In cross-examination, Mr Tucker sought the opinion of the witness as to his brother's general behaviour. In answer, he described his elder brother as a steady and cheerful man who bore a good character. When asked if his brother and the deceased always got on well together, he nodded his head, then, with a half-smile said 'I could not say that, sir. He was not easily put into a bad temper, but when he was roused, it took a lot to quell.' Lastly, Mr Tucker asked 'When he came in, did he say that he thought he had 'done a woman in'?' His emphatic reply was 'No, sir, he said "I've done her in!"'

Police Constable John Pinxton deposed that Edward Leatherland entered Hill Top police station at 12.20 a.m. on Monday 20 September, accompanied by his younger brother, Joseph. The prisoner declared 'Put the handcuffs on me, Mr Pinxton, I have done a murder.' When asked what his response was, Constable Pinxton replied 'I said, "No, you're quiet enough. What's all that blood on your shirt and your hands?"' The prisoner then said, 'I've done Sarah Brookes in.' Leatherland smelt of alcohol, but, in the opinion of Constable Pinxton, was quite sober.

During Sergeant Benton's description of the murder scene on discovery of the body, one by one, dozens of gruesome exhibits were shown to the jury, including bloodstained furnace cinders and stones, as well as the shattered remains of the two beer bottles carried by the couple that fateful night. Throughout this macabre display, Leatherland sat with his eyes turned away to the floor. When the sergeant produced Leatherland's signed statement made at Hill Top police station that night, the judge inquired as to how it had become bloodstained. The reply was that they had come from the prisoner's unwashed hands.

The final evidence put before the jury consisted of the results of medical and pathological examinations carried out by Dr Thomas Heywood Sansome and Professor Charles H. Wilson. In describing the victim's injuries, Dr Sansome pointed out on his own head and face the position of the blows. He concluded that the cause of death was shock, resultant from the severity of the injuries.

Dr Sansome went on to describe how Leatherland had visited his surgery on the Thursday previous, 16 September, and was examined upon the prisoner's request, and found to be suffering from acute venereal disease. When cross-examined by Mr Tucker, the doctor said that when told of his condition, the prisoner became very upset. 'What generally is the effect of this disease upon a man's mind?' asked Mr Tucker. 'It depends upon the man,' replied Dr Sansome. 'May not this particular disease affect the man's mind and make it unbalanced?' asked the barrister, to which the doctor answered 'Certain diseases do have an effect upon the mind, but not this one.'

'May it not have made him depressed?' asked Mr Tucker

'Yes.'

'Especially if the man had previously borne a good character?' persisted Mr Tucker

'Yes.' replied Dr Sansome.

That remained for Professor Wilson to confirm that examination of the deceased's genital organs, sent to him by Dr Sansome, proved that she also had been suffering from the same condition.

For his defence, Leatherland was put into the witness box by Mr Tucker, where he gave his evidence very clearly. He said that he had known Sarah Brookes for two years but in recent months had become more intimate with her, and that misconduct had taken place frequently. Subsequently, he went to see Dr Sansome and when told what was the matter with him, he became very upset.

Referring to the evening when they travelled back from Wolverhampton together on the train, Leatherland said that after leaving the railway station at Wednesbury, they had four or five pints of ale together at a public house, and at closing time, be brought a couple of sealed bottles away to consume later. They walked up Holloway Bank and entered the field known as the Hilly-Piece. There, they sat down and Leatherland said:

> I made up my mind to tell her what she had given me. I said to her 'do you realise what you have given me?' She snarled and threw her head back as if to express that she didn't care. I said 'Do you realise that you have ruined my life? I have a mind to give you a good hiding.' I pulled the razor from my pocket, intending to do myself in, and she made a grab for it, knocking it from my hand. I said to her again 'Do you realise what you have done for me?' Then I lost my head. I used the cinder and the bottles, but I hardly knew what I did then.

Mr Tucker asked 'Did you ever intend to kill her?'

'No, sir.' replied the prisoner. Cross-examined by Mr Morrison, Leatherland admitted that, when told by Dr Sansome what was the matter with him, he was very angry about Sarah Brookes. 'Why did you not avoid her?' asked Mr Morrison.

'I thought it was my duty to explain it to her.' was his reply. He denied that he took the razor with him for the purpose of killing her.

In reply to the judge asking why alternative weapons were used, he said he broke both the bottles over the woman's head before he used the furnace cinder, but he hardly knew what he was doing. Mr Morrison submitted to the jury that it was an act of revenge committed in a fit of passion for what the deceased woman had given him. In the prisoner's defence, Mr Tucker agreed that the killing was the result of a sudden passion caused by the thought of the disease which this woman had given him, but urged the jury to see that there was no malice and no intent to kill.

The judge began his summing up with a dramatic recital of the dead woman's injuries. 'The victim' he said 'of murder most foul and cruel and brutal.' He reviewed the evidence, paying particular attention to the argument as to whether this particular disease had disturbed the balance of the prisoner's mind, pointing out that it had not prevented him forming the intent to confront the woman with his complaint to carry out the deed, and to later surrender to the police. He said:

> By the law of this country, a person was presumed to intend what – in fact – he did. If a man struck a woman on the head and she died as a result of it, the burden was on the defence to satisfy the jury that the man's mind was not capable of forming an intention at the time.

With that, the jury were invited to retire and consider their verdict. They were secreted in a private room at 1.50 p.m. and returned into court an hour and five

*The Hilly-Piece today. (Author's collection)*

minutes later. When asked by the Clerk of Court if they had agreed upon a verdict, the whole jury nodded or murmured in assent, the foreman adding, 'We find the prisoner guilt of manslaughter, sir.'

The judge then addressed Leatherland saying, 'The jury have taken a very merciful view of the case. I do not say that they are wrong; I am far from suggesting it; but a more wicked, cruel manslaughter I have never met with before in all my life. The sentence of the court is that you be sent to penal servitude for fifteen years.'

On hearing the sentence, Leatherland turned round to scan the public gallery, possibly in search of his parents. From the back, a young woman waved to him. One thing seemed sure; there would be no shortage of prison visitors for the next fifteen years, with plenty of willing suitors lined up for his freedom beyond.

Today, the poverty stricken slums of Rydding Square are long since gone, extended and replaced with a pleasant open-plan development, its comfortable homes a far cry from the conditions suffered by the families of Matilda Coleyshaw and Sarah Brookes. Ironically, the remaining portion of the Hilly-Piece, a grassy area of public open space between Hampshire road and Crookhay Lane, is a place where children innocently play and courting couples stroll together, blissfully unaware of the dark history of its lush green acres.

# 8

# JEREMIAH HANBURY'S REVENGE

## *Brockmoor, 1932*

The ecclesiastical parish of Brockmoor lies barely half a mile north-west of its larger neighbour Brierley Hill, into whose Urban District it was absorbed in 1934. Previously, this domain of foundries and brickyards, juxtaposed with an intermittent scatter of working-class residential quarters, came under the administration of Kingswinford Rural District Council.

One such residential quarter was Newtown, a narrow lane leading from Brockmoor High Street to a straggle of quaint, though somewhat impoverished, nineteenth-century cottages adjacent to the burial ground of St John's Church. Here, at No. 18, one of a row of five dwellings sharing a communal yard, resided Jeremiah Hanbury, a widower, who had lived alone for the past four years.

A puddler by trade, as a teenager he took employment at Bromley Ironworks, moving later to Messrs Brown & Freer, where, following closure in 1920, the Leys estate council housing development was built. He continued in ironfounding for a while, working at the Earl of Dudley's Round Oak Works, Brierley Hill, before taking casual labouring jobs at local building sites, the last being two years before on the Nagersfield Road scheme in nearby Hawbush.

Now aged forty-nine in 1932, he was unemployed with much spare time on his hands. Some of this time was spent making regular daytime visits to the Leys Crescent home of attractive housewife Jessie Payne, aged thirty-nine, with whom he had been conducting an affair since the death of his wife. A mother of four young children, Mrs Payne and her husband James Charles, known as Charlie, had lived in Station Road, Brockmoor, prior to being allocated their new council home.

*The entrance to Newtown, Brockmoor, showing St John's Church. (Author's collection)*

*Leys Crescent, Brockmoor. (Author's collection)*

*Jeremiah Hanbury. (Courtesy of Sandwell Community History and Archive Service)*

Mr Payne, who was employed as a lorry driver at the Dudley & Blower's Green Motor Transport Co. Ltd, met his wife of fifteen years through a wartime romance. Whilst serving abroad in the South Staffordshire Regiment, he was brought home suffering from frostbitten feet, and was sent to the Royal Infirmary, Manchester, where his wife-to-be was a probationer nurse. A native of Chorley, Lancashire, her family, the Pearsons, were salt merchants in Manchester. Mr Payne had two brothers living in the locality; William resided in Cottage Lane, Brockmoor, and Frederick, 2 miles away at Pensnett.

Jeremiah Hanbury had a stepson, serving in the armed forces, and two stepdaughters, Lily was married and living in Wordsley, a few miles distance, with the younger sister lodging at the same address. His niece, Sarah Pratt, would check on him daily, being just a short walk away at No. 18 Cressett Lane, Brockmoor. She was very much aware of her uncle's misconduct, and that Jessie Payne was a married woman.

On 22 June, Detective Constable Chadwick and Sergeant Lea, both stationed at Brierley Hill, called at the Payne household whilst making enquiries into an unlawful abortion case, Mrs Payne's name having been mentioned in connection with the matter. The officers arranged to take statements from the couple the following day. As they left the property, Jeremiah Hanbury entered through the garden gate, making one of his regular social calls on Charlie Payne. The unsuspecting man had known Hanbury all his life and such was their friendship that he regarded the widower almost as a third brother.

This was to be one of Hanbury's last visits to Leys Crescent, for rather abruptly at the beginning of July, Mrs Payne ended her liaison with him, forbidding his return to her family home. Immediately, his anger was kindled. With a hurt pride, he began to publicly denounce his former mistress, telling one of her neighbours:

Jessie has turned me away from her front door. She has been my wife regularly these past four years. She has been having from me 15 to 16s per week. Now she has given me up because there is someone else who has more money than me. When she turned me away from her door it was as bad as when I buried my wife. I shall have my revenge on both her and him.

Hanbury did not disclose the name of his love rival for whom he alleged Mrs Payne had cast him aside.

One day, early in September, whilst walking home from visiting his brother in Cottage Lane, Mr Payne was stopped by Hanbury, who demanded to know why he was banned from calling at his Leys Crescent home. He replied that it was his wife's decision, but she would not tell him why. Hanbury then said, 'Well this has got to be cleared up first and last'. Asked what was meant by those words, Hanbury mischievously suggested, 'If you will go to your house unexpectedly sometime, you will see for yourself,' adding, 'Go on down to your place and tell Jessie what I have just said.' When confronted by her husband, Mrs Payne confessed to misconducting with Hanbury, but only the once, insisting that she had been forced in the matter.

On 3 October, Detective Constable Chadwick was visiting the Alma Inn, Mill Street, Brierley Hill, when the landlord indicated that Jeremiah Hanbury wished to speak with him in the rear yard. There he was told, 'Do you remember going to Payne's house about stopping kids? Well she did stop one. She told you all lies, it was my kid. I have been misconducting myself with her these last four years, and paying for it. Now the money has gone she has stopped me.' Then chillingly he warned, 'But I shall make her suffer. I will find you such a big job one of these days.'

Hanbury spoke again with Charlie Payne when the pair met on 8 October at the Brockmoor House Inn, Station Road. Mr Payne told him that his wife had denied she had a long affair, confessing to misconducting on only one occasion.

*The Brockmoor House Inn, seen years earlier when affected by mining subsidence. (Coutesy of Stan Hill)*

Hanbury insisted that they had been involved in clandestine meetings all the time since his wife had died, and that Mrs Payne regularly accepted money from him. He told his friend, 'Your wife has been a bad woman. I can go home with your wife anytime I choose.' Mr Payne remonstrated with Hanbury, saying, 'I have four lovely children and a nice home which I don't want broken up. Leave it drop and let me live it down.'

It was a plea that fell on deaf ears. Hanbury grew more bitter by the day as he festered over Jessie Payne's rejection of him. He became a haunted man, telling his niece, 'You don't understand how I feel. I cannot sleep in bed at night. She has thrown me over for someone else and I cannot forget her. She is calling to me all the while.' On Friday 14 October in another conversation with Alice Baker, he became more sinister, saying, 'I love her so, that if she had said to me, "Murder Charlie Payne", I should have murdered him so we could be together. That is what it has come to.' On this occasion he was almost in tears.

By the morning of Monday 17 October, starved of sleep and his anger at a climax, his tortured mind resolved to take action. Whilst he cobbled three pairs of boots for a neighbour, slicing through leather and hammering in hobnails, his gentle dexterity gave over to brute force. Today Jessie Payne would receive one final and fatal visit from Jeremiah Hanbury. Leaving home at 1.15 p.m., his trademark black scarf wrapped around his neck, he first headed towards the Brockmoor House Inn to take some 'Dutch courage', ready for his planned confrontation with the woman who had shunned him.

Half an hour later, he was seen by a friend, Edward Simpson, walking at a hurried pace along Brockmoor High Street in the direction of the Leys estate. He had his right hand tucked inside his right coat pocket. He never spoke, but stared straight ahead, wearing a savage expression upon his face. Well aware of the couple's habits, he knew that Charlie Payne would have returned to work at 1.30 p.m. following his lunchbreak, and now his wife would be alone inside the house, their four children safely away at school.

There is a long tradition amongst the working classes that Monday is given over to washing the laundry; the Black Country is no exception. At 2.05 p.m., Edith Elizabeth Harris was pegging out the last of her washing and noticed her next-door neighbour, Mrs Payne, shaking a tablecloth in her back garden, evidently clearing up after lunch. Mrs Harris went back inside her house for about five minutes, but when she returned to the garden was surprised to see Jeremiah Hanbury leaving the Payne's house by the rear door. She had not noticed him enter. He turned to her and said, 'Come on, I have done it now.' His coat and shirt were torn open, and he was spattered all over with blood. More oozed from a deep incision in his throat. Mrs Harris clasped her chest and let out a loud scream.

On hearing this, neighbour Mr Frank Hill, who was upstairs, raced down and into his garden, which backed onto that of the Payne's. Other neighbours too were alerted by the commotion and also witnessed Hanbury leaving the Payne residence covered with blood. He told Priscilla Edmunds, watching from her backyard,

'You can go to her now; I have done it.' He spoke in an ordinary calm voice but had a wild look about him. As he walked to the front of the house, he told a bystander, Maria Bate, 'I have done her in', then casually went on his way, back towards Brockmoor High Street.

Hysterically, Mrs Harris told Mr Hill what she had just witnessed. He walked to the back door of the Payne's house, which stood half open. On entering, he met with the most terrible sight. Mrs Payne lay fully clothed on her back, sprawled across the kitchen floor. Blood poured rapidly from a gaping wound in her throat, forming an ever-growing crimson pool around her body. Her head was tilted slightly to the right side and almost severed from her body. Mr Hill called out her name, but unsurprisingly got no reply. He noticed that her top dental plate was broken in two and protruded through the lips. The right side of her forehead bore a brutally inflicted wound.

Nine inches from the body, near to the kitchen sink, lay a bloodstained hammer, its shaft pointing away from the victim. Strands of Mrs Payne's hair were adhered to the head of the weapon. A half-open cut-throat razor, also bloodied, was positioned 3in to the right of where she came to rest, her body parallel with the kitchen window. Hanbury's black scarf was loosely gripped by the fingers of her right hand and trailed away from the body. Artificial pearls littered the floor, strewn in all directions. This then was Jeremiah Hanbury's method of threatened revenge. Mr Hill kept guard at the house while other neighbours saw to alerting the police. Quickly on the scene were Constables Hazell and J. Green, as was the vicar of nearby St John's Church, the Revd G.W. Milward, who immediately proceeded to administer the last rites to the dying woman.

Meanwhile, Jeremiah Hanbury was the centre of all attention as his dishevelled and blood spattered figure ambled along Brockmoor High Street. Edward Simpson, who had seen the deranged man heading towards the Leys thirty minutes earlier, was now in

conversation with an associate. His companion stopped Hanbury and exclaimed, 'Whatever have you been doing, Jerry?' to which he simply replied, 'Murder.' His complexion was near white and he appeared totally unaware of the self-inflicted trauma to his throat. Mr Simpson reiterated, 'Good God, Jerry, what have you been doing?' Hanbury raised his hands level with his shoulders and held his palms outwards. He jerked his head backwards in the direction of the Leys and said, 'Murder, murder, down there.'

*Jessie Payne. (Courtesy of Sandwell Community History and Archive Service)*

At 2.20 p.m., he passed Louisa Phoebe Marsh, who had just left her home, No. 52 High Street, and was walking in the direction of the Leys. Although he knew the woman well, he did not seem to recognise her. As he walked by, she heard him mutter, 'Jerry said revenge. Jerry's had revenge.' He then turned the corner near her house and headed towards his own home in Newtown. Looking through her window at No. 17 was his next-door neighbour, Mrs Alice Emery. She saw Hanbury cross the yard and stand on his doorstep, turning the lock. He entered his cottage but left again only moments later, locking the door again behind him.

Above and below: *Two views of Brockmoor High Street, 1932. (Courtesy of Michael Reuter)*

Seeing her gazing out, he appeared at her window and endeavoured to speak. Mrs Emery came outside and asked him what the matter was. It was only then that she noticed his hands and the front of his clothes were saturated in blood. He called to her, 'Alice, come here, don't be afraid. I am not going to hurt you.'

'What have you been doing?' asked the shocked woman.

'I have killed Jessie Payne with a razor,' he replied. Her attention was then drawn to the horrific wound in his throat. Alarmed, she stammered, 'Good heavens, Jerry, what have you done that with?' Now choking, he gasped, 'With a razor; I've done it. Go and tell Sarah and Lily.' He muttered that he had left an explanation note in his cottage, before leaving the yard, still bleeding profusely.

Hanbury next encountered James Henry Round, a man he knew very well, who was walking along Brockmoor High Street towards Newtown. Noticing his injury and blood all over his clothing, Mr Round enquired, 'Well, Jerry. What have you been up to?' Still speaking in his usual tone, and as if about some ordinary matter, Hanbury answered, 'I have done a murder.' Leaving Mr Round standing with his mouth open, he continued up High Street and turned left into Hickman Road where at No. 2 lived another associate, Elijah Watts.

Mr Watts had just returned home from his work as a baker, and, as was his usual routine, had been checking his pigsties at the rear of his property. His livestock inspected, he walked to the front of his house and saw Jeremiah Hanbury heading in his direction. As Hanbury moved closer, Mr Watts realised that blood was pouring from his throat. He shouted, 'What's the matter, Jerry? What have you done?' Hanbury held his bloodstained hands to his face and cried, 'I've cut it. I have cut my throat with a razor.'

Hanbury then caught sight of Police Constable Kirkham cycling at speed towards him. Ironically, he was answering his superiors call to attend the awful incident at the Payne household. Hanbury walked out into the middle of the road, waving his left arm to the officer, beckoning him to stop. As Constable Kirkham dismounted from his bicycle, Hanbury blurted, 'Come on, something terrible has happened. I have killed her. I was coming over to your place to give myself up.'

Elijah Watts rushed up to Hanbury's side to prevent his collapse and, with Constable Kirkham, almost carried him up his garden path and to the rear of the house where they laid him down. The Brierley Hill motor ambulance was sent for and in the meantime, Constable Kirkham rendered first aid to Hanbury's throat, and also the index finger of his right hand, out of which was cut an oval-shaped piece of flesh.

Presently, his niece, Sarah Pratt, joined them. Having been informed of the tragedy by her uncle's neighbour, Mrs Emery, she followed the trail of blood to Elijah Watts' house. He appeared dazed and held his arms outstretched while she cradled his head like a baby. She kissed him and in return, he shook her hand. She gently asked, 'What have you done?' and he replied, 'I don't know.' She asked 'Where have you done it?' Again he replied, 'I don't know.' She pleaded, 'What have you done it with?' but again he just replied the same.

His memory appeared to return when he was cautioned by Constable Kirkham, for he declared:

> I killed Mrs Payne. I know I did some way. I have done one thing, I came out. I could not live without her. You remember what I was telling you police about getting out of those children? She told a pack of lies, she has that. I know all about it. Never mind if I do get hung. I shall only get hung once. This job never ought to have happened. She's a wrong one. I have relieved this world of a heap of trouble.

Now Sergeant Lea from Brierley Hill police station arrived to take charge of Hanbury. At 2.45 p.m., Dr E. Wentworth Moore was summoned to Hickman Road and examined Hanbury's injured throat, of which Constable Kirkham had been stemming the flow of blood. It was a serious wound which had cut some blood vessels and the windpipe, the incision being 5in long and ½in deep. Hanbury had lost a moderate amount of blood. He was placed in the motor ambulance, driven by Mr Ebenezer Beckley, and conveyed to the infirmary at Sandfield House, Wordsley. Throughout the journey, he was escorted by Sergeant Lea and Constable Kirkham. Dr Moore then left the scene and headed towards the Leys estate.

On the way, the ambulance halted outside the Payne's house, and Sergeant Lea went inside to collect the pad of Hanbury's sliced finger which had been recovered from the kitchen floor. During his absence, Hanbury turned to his escort and said, 'You have always been a good one, Kirkham.' As Sergeant Lea got back into the ambulance, he was asked:

> Is she dead? I'll never tell lies. I was never a coward in my life. I have always liked to be straight with one another. I must have been off my stupid head when I went into that house. I don't remember now. I know I did it, but I don't know what with.

At Sandfield House, Hanbury had eighteen stitches inserted into his throat wound, and remained under the charge of Sergeant Lea and constable Kirkham. He told the constable, 'I said to her, "Why don't your husband stop me from coming here instead of you?" It would not look so bad.' He then asked, 'Is she knocked about a bit? From after two o'clock I killed her, but I can't remember using a razor. I don't know how I have done this. My niece thought that you were going to set about me when you got off your bike.'

He told Sergeant Lea:

> Come here; you know why I have done this. I have almost been living with Jessie Payne, everything, but sleeping there until about ten weeks ago, when another bloke started going there and she stopped me. That is the cause of all this trouble. I took the razor with me, but I don't remember what I did with it. I don't know if I killed her with it or not. Is she knocked about a lot? After two o'clock I killed her.

Back in Leys Crescent, the Payne's house was a hive of activity. Dr G. Keith Gifford had raced from his Moor Street surgery, but, the poor woman was beyond medical assistance, and all he could do was to pronounce life to be extinct. Dr E. Wentworth Moore proceeded to conduct the necessary medical examination of the body, as found, in preparation for the post-mortem. Superintendent Elliott of Brierley Hill Police arrived to oversee the murder investigation. Professional photographer, Charles Dunn, was sent for from his studio at No. 34 High Street, Brierley Hill and tasked with capturing on film the gory images of the victim, surrounded by the murder weapons on the blood-soaked kitchen floor in four dramatic exposures.

Once this assignment was undertaken, the body was then carefully removed from the kitchen floor and stretchered to an awaiting hearse for the journey to Brierley Hill District Mortuary. A waiting group of tearful neighbours bowed their heads in grim silence as Jessie Payne's mortal remains were driven away at a dignified pace.

Surveyor Frank Vincent Williams was now busily engaged in measuring up the kitchen and precincts of the Payne household, and also surrounding footpaths to neighbouring properties, ready to produce a detailed plan to be used as evidence later in court. Apart from the masses of blood on the kitchen floor, the house presented a very tidy appearance.

On inspection, Superintendent Elliott observed that the lunchtime utensils had been washed up and put away. Upstairs, the beds were all made up for the end of the day. There was even a favourite doll placed on the pillow of one of the beds, ready no doubt, for the youngest child to be safely tucked up later that night. Outside, there were no signs of the slaughter, except for some bloodied fingerprints on the gate and wooden fencing.

Later in the afternoon, the victim's four young children were collected from school and taken to the home of a relative, Mrs Phillips, at No. 72 Fenton Street, Brockmoor. Charlie Payne, now a widower, was a pitiful sight as he was brought back to his home in his works manager's car at 4.30 p.m. His distress was all too obvious to see as he was met by Superintendent Elliott and led inside the house.

The following day, Mr Payne made a formal identification of his wife's body at the mortuary prior to commencement of the post-mortem examination, which was carried out by Dr E. Wentworth Moore. In his report, he stated that during the autopsy, he discovered additional injuries that he had not previously noticed when viewing the body on the kitchen floor of the victim's home the day before.

To the back of the skull there was a cut over the occipital bone, underneath which he found a depressed fracture, caused in all probability by the hammer found on the kitchen floor with strands of Mrs Payne's hair attached to it. Just above this injury was a severe contusion, consistent with a sudden violent fall to the ground. At the front of the skull there was another severe bruise to the right side of her forehead. No fracture was found beneath this wound, which again, was probably delivered with the hammer. Either one of these two blows could have rendered her unconscious. In the doctor's opinion, the blows to the head preceded the cutting of the throat.

*James Charles Payne. (Courtesy of Sandwell Community History and Archive Service)*

The incision to the throat was 7½in long, superficial on the left side but very deep to the right. Main blood vessels, the jugular vein, and the muscles of the neck had all been completely severed. The woman died of haemorrhage due to the severity of the throat wound. Death would have ensued within three to five minutes of the injury being inflicted. He examined the heart and found it to be healthy but completely emptied of blood. The lungs though, showed signs of previous bronchitis and also pleural adhesions.

In the afternoon, following Mr Payne's formal identification of his wife, one of her sisters arrived by train from Manchester and joined her stricken brother-in-law in visiting her poor nieces and nephews, being suitably cared for in Fenton Street. After assisting in the formalities of registering the death and preliminary funeral arrangements, she left Brockmoor for her return journey north.

At Brierley Hill police station on Wednesday 19 October, the inquest into Mrs Payne's horrific death was opened by the county coroner, Mr J.T. Higgs. The coroner's jury consisted of: Mr Charles Ansell (foreman), with Messrs J. Downing, H.W. Griffiths, A.D. Robinson, S.E. Williams, E.J. Adey, T. Beaman, J. Hutt and E. Browne. The jury, rather understandably, elected not to view the body. After hearing evidence of identification from Charlie Payne, Mr Higgs informed the jury that he proposed to issue a burial order for the funeral to take place.

He explained that a post-mortem examination had taken place, and that the report by the medical officer, Dr Moore, was in his possession, but he did not propose to go further with the inquiry that day, because there was a likelihood that a charge would be preferred against someone relating to the death of the woman. Therefore, it was only right that this person should have the opportunity of being present at the inquest. After consulting with Superintendent Elliott and the members of the jury, the coroner adjourned the inquest until 2 November, commenting to the jurors that 'adjournment would only be a short matter'.

On Saturday 22 October at 12 noon, the distinctive firebrick-built parish church of St John was 'filled to the rafters' with family, friends, and as many of the near 4,500 parishioners who could be seated to pay their last respects to Mrs Jessie Payne. The funeral service was conducted by the vicar of Brockmoor, the Revd Kenneth G.W. Milward.

When Hanbury was sufficiently recovered from his injuries, Superintendent Elliott cautioned the man before reading the murder charge, to which he bluntly replied, 'I don't remember nothing of it.' He was then removed to Birmingham's Winson Green Prison, pending a series of remands, culminating with the committal hearing at Brierley Hill Police Court on Wednesday 16 November.

Several hundred people had waited outside the court building to catch a glimpse of Hanbury being escorted from the prison van on arrival from Winson Green. No one from the general public was admitted to the courtroom, which was also cleared of all witnesses just before the case was opened. The magistrates were Mr Sydney George Dudley JP (chairman), and Mr William Pearson JP. Mr O. Barnett conducted the case for the prosecution, and Mr J.F. Bourke, instructed by Messrs Waldron & Son, solicitors, of Brierley Hill, represented the accused.

In opening the case, Mr Barnett said:

On 17 October, shortly after 2 p.m., Mrs Jessie Payne was murdered. Her throat was cut, and she died of haemorrhage. She had also received two violent blows to the skull from some heavy instrument, about which the court shall hear later. Minutes afterwards, a Mrs Harris saw Jeremiah Hanbury leave Mrs Payne's house. She noticed that he had blood pouring from a throat wound and he said, 'Come on; I have done it now.' Hanbury went around the corner and turned into a passage up the main road. He was a man Mrs Harris knew quite well, and he often visited Mrs Payne's house. He had in fact been a frequent visitor, but she had not seen him there so much recently.

*The Leys estate. (Author's collection)*

He told the court that in total, eight witnesses would be called who had encountered Hanbury between 2.10 p.m. and 2.30 p.m. on that fateful afternoon, and had heard him make various statements such as, 'Come on, I have done it now,' and 'I have done murder.' Other witnesses would include the husband of the deceased, and various medical officers and police officers.

Continuing with his outline of the case, Mr Barnett said:

A Mr Hill, who lives on the Leys estate heard a scream and rushed to Mrs Payne's house. The back door was half open and he saw a large quantity of blood on the floor. He went inside and saw Mrs Payne lying on her back with a terrible wound in her throat. She appeared to be dead, and when he spoke to her he could get no answer. Police Constable Kirkham saw Hanbury in Hickman Road. Hanbury said to him, 'Come on, something terrible has happened. I have killed her,' adding, 'I was coming down to your place to give myself up.' Hanbury at that time had a self-inflicted wound in his throat which was bleeding profusely, and his clothing was covered in blood. The constable placed him behind a house in Hickman Road, and rendered first aid. Other police officers were called, and after being cautioned, Hanbury said, 'I killed Mrs Payne. I know I did some way.' Later, he made a statement in which he said Mrs Payne had told him a pack of lies. Hanbury's windpipe was badly cut, and he was taken to the infirmary, following which, other police officers went to Mrs Payne's house.

Mr Barnett then told of the murder weapons, saying:

They found a razor and hammer lying close to the woman's head. Both were covered with blood, and there was hair adhering to the hammer which corresponded to that of Mrs Payne. There was also a black scarf in the room which had been identified as belonging to Hanbury. Dr Moore made a post-mortem examination of the body, and will tell this court that her injuries must have been caused with the weapons found on the kitchen floor, which in turn, will be proven to belong to the accused.

The first witness to give evidence was Jessie Payne's next-door neighbour, Mrs Edith Elizabeth Harris. She told of seeing Hanbury leave Mrs Payne's house, and turning to her, covered in blood, indicate he had done something to Mrs Payne. 'He was not hurrying, but was leaving the house in quite an ordinary way', she said. She told the hearing that the last occasion she had seen Hanbury there was about three months before.

Cross-examined by Mr Bourke, she said:

In those three months, I had only seen the accused to pass the time of day. Before that, he had been a visitor to the Payne's house almost daily, and usually while Mr Payne was away at work. He would be in the house alone with Mrs Payne for a considerable period of time. I didn't know that they were misconducting themselves. Mrs Payne seemed to me to be a very respectable woman.

In answer to Mr Bourke, she said that the accused was very well known to her, but he had not explained why his visits to her neighbours had suddenly stopped. She added, 'When he used the words "Come on", I understood that he wanted me to go into the Payne's house. His tone was ordinary, as though he was speaking about something quite unimportant.' She heard no screams or conversation come from the Payne's house.

Neighbour, Mrs Priscilla Edmunds, told of standing in her back garden, and seeing Hanbury come out through Mrs Payne's back door. 'He looked like his normal self,' she said, 'but his shirt was open and he was bleeding from the throat, and there was blood on his hands.' In reply to Mr Bourke, she stated that she was standing about 20yds away and could see Hanbury quite clearly. She also heard him speak to Mrs Harris, who did not reply, but only screamed.

Maria Bate said she was visiting her sister-in-law at Leys Crescent, when she saw Hanbury leave Mrs Payne's house. She explained, 'He looked rather wild, his coat and shirt were open and he had a cut in his throat about 5in long. He said, "I have done her in", and then went along the path to the front of the house. He had got nothing around his neck.' Mr Bourke asked her to describe Hanbury's appearance, and she said, 'He looked like a madman, and talked as if he was so mad he didn't know what he was saying.'

Mr Edward Simpson, a motor driver, of the Leys estate, and well known to Hanbury and the Paynes, told the court that at 1.45 p.m. on 17 October, he saw Hanbury walking along Brockmoor High Street towards the Leys estate. Hanbury had his right hand tucked into his right coat pocket, as if concealing something, and seemed to be in an awful hurry. He never spoke and looked as if he had got a savage expression upon his face. 'About thirty minutes later,' said Mr Simpson, 'I was talking to a friend when Hanbury came back along High Street, covered in blood and with his throat cut. I asked, "Good God, Jerry, what have you been doing?", and he replied ,"Murder, murder, down there." As he spoke, he gestured towards Leys Crescent.'

Cross-examined by Mr Bourke, he said:

> I know Jeremiah Hanbury very well, and on both occasions was amazed at his behaviour. I though his remarks, in a way, were those of a madman. His face was very white and as far as I could see, was unaware of the injury to this throat. I watched as he headed along Newtown, and then came back and turned towards Hickman Road.

Louisa Phoebe Marsh told of leaving her house in Brockmoor High Street and walking towards the Leys estate. She saw Hanbury heading in her direction and although they had known each other for several years, he did not speak directly to her, nor seemed to notice her or the wound to his throat. As he passed by, she heard him mutter the words, 'Jerry said revenge. Jerry's had revenge.'

Next to give evidence was Hanbury's next-door neighbour, Mrs Alice Emery. She said:

Jerry, as we call him, came into the yard shortly after 2.20 p.m. I did not notice the blood at first until a neighbour's little boy called out to his father, 'Look, father, Jerry has been run over or something.' He entered his house, but came out again almost immediately afterwards and locked the front door. Then he noticed me looking through the window and beckoned me outside. I asked what the matter was and he replied, 'I have killed Jessie Payne with a razor.' He was more like a wild man than anything else.

James Henry Round, of No. 47 Hulland, Brockmoor, said that he knew the accused very well. 'At about 2.30 p.m., I met Jerry in High Street, and noticing his condition asked; "Well, Jerry, what have you been up to?" He replied, "I have done a murder!" Blood was coming from his throat and was all over his clothes.' Mr Round told the court. In reply to Mr Bourke, he added, 'Jerry spoke in his usual voice as though mentioning an ordinary matter, and as if he had no injury of his own.'

Hanbury's friend, Elijah Watts, told of returning to his home at No. 2 Hickman Road shortly after 2.30 p.m. and after first inspecting his livestock, encountering Hanbury at the front of his house. He described Hanbury's appearance as that of a 'painted man', so covered in blood he was. Cross-examined by Mr Bourke, he said, 'Jerry did not seem to be the same man the last six or seven weeks before 17 October. He always seemed to be troubled in some way.' When shown the razor, recovered from the kitchen floor at the Payne's house, he agree that it belonged to Hanbury who had lent it to him once whilst his own was being sharpened.

Constable Kirkham, stationed at Brockmoor, said:

A little after 2.30 p.m. on Monday 17 October, I was cycling towards the Payne's house, answering an urgent call. As I was going down Hickman Road, I saw the accused walking in the centre of the road towards me. He flagged me down by waving his left arm as a signal to stop. When I got up to him, I noticed that his coat and shirt front were open. He was covered in blood and bleeding profusely from a wound in the throat. The accused then said, 'Come on, something terrible has happened. I have killed her. I was coming over to your place to give myself up.' I took him to the rear of No. 2 Hickman Road and rendered first aid to his throat and also to the first finger of his right hand. An oval shaped piece of flesh was cut out of the pad of the finger.

During cross-examination by Mr Bourke, the officer agreed that Hanbury was walking in the direction of the police station.

Hanbury's niece, Mrs Sarah Pratt, said she was in the habit of looking after her uncle since the death of his wife. She told the court that several years ago, he had threatened many times to 'do away with himself'. His trouble at that time was a disappointment about a failed love affair. He used to get up in the night, and had to be restrained. Later, he was married, during which time all seemed to be well, but after his wife died, he began to associate with Mrs Payne. 'He seemed to be going "loony"', said Mrs Pratt, regarding his troubles with the woman, adding, 'I had a very bad dream on the Sunday night before and I expected something terrible to happen.'

Of the murder scene, Police Constable Hazel described how he answered an emergency call to the Payne's house, and discovered the victim's body on the kitchen floor, lying parallel to the window in a pool of blood. She was fully dressed, wearing indoor clothes. She had a long, deep wound in the neck. Her top dental plate had been broken and pieces of it protruded through her lips. He searched the room and found a piece of flesh, the size of which seemed to correspond with that missing from the accused's finger. While he was present, four photographs were taken of the gruesome scene.

Describing the results of his post-mortem examination, Dr E. Wentworth Moore deposed that the two wounds to the scalp were consistent with being hit by a hard, compact instrument, such as the hammer recovered from the kitchen floor. Hairs adhering to the bloodstained tool matched those on the head of the victim. The doctor was satisfied that none of the injuries could have been self-inflicted. In reply to Mr Bourke, he admitted that he could not say whether either of the head wounds alone would have been fatal.

The victim's husband, James Charles Payne, told of returning to work at 1.30 p.m. on Monday 17 October, after spending his lunchtime at home with his wife. When he left, she was in good spirits and perfect health. Later in the afternoon, he was summoned home by the police, arriving there at 4.30 p.m. Inside the house, he was asked to identify a razor and hammer, but had never seen them in his home before. They did not belong to him, and were certainly not in the house when he left for work at 1.30 p.m.

The black scarf, however, he identified as belonging to Jeremiah Hanbury. He had seen him wearing it on many occasions previously. Mr Payne said that Hanbury had been a frequent visitor to his home, and he had known him all his life. He was very friendly with his wife, and he trusted him to be alone with her. Often, when he called back home during working hours, Hanbury would be there. Mr Payne then spoke of identifying his wife's injured body at Brierley Hill District Mortuary the following day.

Then, in a strange twist, under cross-examination, Mr Payne admitted that on one evening before the tragedy, Hanbury came to their front door, and in his wife's presence, told him what had been going on between them. She, though, denied it. Mr Bourke asked, 'Did Hanbury go so far as to complain that someone else had taken his place?'

'No,' replied Mr Payne. Mr Bourke then handed him a piece of paper to read, asking, 'Did he mention that man's name?' Again, Mr Payne replied in the negative. The alleged love rival's name was never disclosed to the court, remaining to this day a secret Jessie Payne took to her grave.

The evidence now all heard, Hanbury was again formally charged with murder and committed to take his trial at Birmingham Winter Assizes. Before concluding the hearing, the Chairman of the Bench, Mr Dudley JP, said that he would like to congratulate Superintendent Elliott upon the excellent manner in which all of the evidence had been collected.

*Birmingham Assize Court. (Author's collection)*

On Thursday 8 December 1932, Prosecuting Counsel, Mr C.B. Marriott KC, opened Hanbury's trial with the words, 'I am afraid I shall have to suggest that this was not only a brutal murder, but also a premeditated one.' In outlining the case, he referred to the savagery of the attack in Mrs Payne's kitchen, saying, 'Nobody saw or heard what took place there, but shortly after 2 p.m., Hanbury was seen to emerge from the house, covered in blood, and Mrs Payne was found on the kitchen floor with her head almost severed from her body.'

The defence was again conducted by Mr J.F. Bourke, and the trial presided over by Mr Justice Humphreys. When James Charles Payne was called to give evidence, it emerged that on the afternoon of the murder, his wife had planned to go to a matinée at a local cinema.

The case for the defence was that at the time of the tragedy, the prisoner was insane. In support of this, Mrs Sarah Pratt insisted that mental affliction ran in her uncle's family. 'His mother once threatened to commit suicide,' she said, 'and following a cycling accident many years ago, he began to act strange when under pressure. For the last three months, he has looked wild and complained that he could not sleep at night.'

Dr G. Chesterfield Cook, of Stourbridge, said that he examined the accused on 28 November, and could find no evidence of insanity. He was, however, suffering from loss of memory of what happened from the time he left the Brockmoor

House Inn on 17 October, until he found himself at the infirmary. 'Loss of memory was sometimes indicative of insanity.' said Dr Cook. In cross-examination, he said that he was of the opinion that Hanbury was insane when he attacked Mrs Payne.

This, though, was challenged by Dr Hamblin Smith, medical officer at Winson Green Prison, Birmingham, and called to give evidence by the Crown. Previously, in reply to the judge, he said that he did not find anything in the facts of the case which led him to think that the accused did not know what he was doing at the time of the murder. He had seen Hanbury daily since his admission to the prison, and had not seen any indication of insanity.

In his summing up, which lasted seventy-five minutes, Mr Justice Humphreys said, 'The simple but grave issue for the jury was; had it been established to their satisfaction by the defence that the accused, at the time he actually killed the woman, due to disease of the mind, did not know what he was doing?' The jury thought not, and after a short deliberation, found Hanbury 'guilty of murder'.

His Lordship turned to Hanbury and asked if he had anything to say why sentence should not be passed upon him. Hanbury sighed deeply, then replied, 'Well, your Lordship, I know nothing about the crime at all. I can't remember anything at all. That is all I have to say.' The judge then placed the black cap upon his head and passed the sentence of death. The attempt by Hanbury's counsel to prove him insane at the time he committed the awful crime had ended in miserable failure.

An application for leave to appeal against the death sentence was immediately lodged. This was brought to the consideration of the Lord Chief Justice, Lord Hewart, on Monday 16 January 1933. Mr P.E. Sandlands appeared for the Crown, whilst the defence remained in the hands of Mr J.F. Bourke. Hanbury stood in the dock, flanked by three prison warders.

Mr Bourke stated that at the trial, held before Mr Justice Humphreys last December, the only defence offered was the plea of insanity, there being no dispute that Hanbury committed the act, and no suggestion of manslaughter. He explained to His Lordship:

On Monday 17 October 1932, Jeremiah Hanbury went to Jessie Payne's house about 2 p.m., and killed her by striking her two violent blows to the head with a hammer. He then cut her throat so deeply that her head was almost severed. He cut his own throat before walking away from the ghastly scene. A short distance away he met a policeman, who took him into custody. It was not disputed that there had been relations between Mrs Payne and Hanbury, but last July, the woman turned him away from her door. This circumstance caused Hanbury to be depressed and worried. One ground of appeal was that the judge, in his summing up, misdirected the jury with regard to the question whether the defendant knew at the time that what he did was wrong. Therefore I submit that there was definite evidence of insanity, from which the jury might have drawn an inference of ignorance of wrong doing, and that was abundant general evidence of insanity.

Lord Hewart pointed out that Hanbury had approached a policeman and said, 'Come on, something terrible has happened. I have killed her. I was coming over to your place to give myself up.' However, Mr Bourke maintained that the judge did not adequately instruct the jury as to the meaning of insanity. His Lordship decided not to call on Mr Sandlands to reply for the Crown. Instead, he upheld the sentence passed on the prisoner, saying:

> The motive for the attack on Mrs Payne was perfectly plain. The motive was that Mrs Payne, who had been co-habiting with Hanbury, had returned to her husband. It was complained by Mr Bourke that there was misdirection by the judge in the sense that he did not direct the jury that they might find Hanbury insane on the grounds that, at the time the crime was committed, he did not know that his actions were unlawful and wrong. It is quite clear this line of defence was fairly put before the jury. In the opinion of Mr Justice Humphreys, there was no evidence to show that Hanbury did not know that what he was doing was wrong. In my opinion the judge was right. There was indeed evidence to show that Hanbury knew he was doing wrong. There is no reason to complain of the judge's summing up and consequently this appeal must be dismissed.

On hearing these words, Hanbury turned and quietly left the dock. He was escorted back to Winson Green Prison, resigned to his fate, with little more to do than count down the days to his impending doom.

# 9

# A SHORTCUT
# TO DEATH

There's not much left of old Moxley today; the sandstone-built All Saints' Church, the former rectory now converted into flats, and between the two, the small limestone war memorial, are the only remaining vestiges of a previously compact village centre, where the roads from Bilston, Wednesbury and Darlaston meet. Way back in 1954, new housing estates were nearing completion, their spacious roads of modern designed homes radiating out beyond the core of early to mid-nineteenth-century buildings where shops, pubs and chapels administered to the daily needs of a growing community.

It was towards this busy centre that three young women, drill machinists, walked at 5 p.m. on Wednesday 1 December, having finished their shifts at Rubery Owen & Co. Ltd, Holyhead Road, Moxley Works. Darkness had fallen as Lilian Joan Collins, Elizabeth Freeman and Joyce Gwendoline Collett chatted happily, joining hundreds of others in a mass exodus from work in an area heavily populated with factories. They entered Moxley along Church Street before Mrs Freeman parted company and turned left towards her home in Queen Street. The other two ladies continued past the Wesleyan chapel in High Street, stopping at the fancy drapery store of Miss Doris Mary French, where Miss Collett said goodbye to her friend and crossed the main road to her home in Burns Place.

Mrs Collins entered the shop where she purchased two ounces of wool and a knitting-pattern book. Afterwards, she quickly called into the village post office and obtained a postal order for 6s from sub-postmistress Gladys Attwood, which was an errand for fellow worker, Mrs Sarah Elizabeth Siverns. She then entered Queen Street where, a little way down, she regularly crossed a piece of wasteland behind

*Church Street, Moxley. The route Lilian Joan Collins walked home from work on the fateful evening of Wednesday 1 December 1954, since made into a duel carriageway. (Author's collection)*

*Looking across the shortcut from Queen Street, Moxley, to Lilian Joan Collins' home in Arden Place (right). (Author's collection)*

*High Street, Moxley, c. 1954. The Wesleyan chapel Sunday school stands on the far left. (Courtesy of All Saints' Church, Moxley)*

the Wesleyan chapel as a shortcut to her widowed mother's home, tucked in a corner of Arden Place where she was staying with two unmarried sisters.

In all, Mrs Cecilia Lloyd had seven daughters. Lilian, aged twenty-five, had married Raymond Collins, a stoker mechanic serving in the Royal Navy, based at Rosyth, Scotland, the previous August, being wed for just under four months. At 5ft 3in tall, with dark hair, she was of an extremely light build and very fragile for a woman of her age, making herself a vulnerable target as she set foot upon the unlit wasteland in gale-force winds. It was now 5.30 p.m.

At 6.15 p.m., one of her four married sisters, Mrs Webb, called at the family home, but found it empty. Other family members returned later, their concern growing when by 9.30 p.m., Lilian still had not arrived home. Her brother, John Lloyd, from nearby Foundry Street, launched a search of the surrounding area, aided by family, friends and neighbours. Shortly after 10 p.m., accompanied by a Mr C. Baldwin, his search took him over the wasteland where approximately 10yds from the rough path and 150yds from the family home, he made the shocking discovery of his sister's body. She was just under a boundary wall at the rear of the Wesleyan chapel, lying on her back with her head facing towards Queen Street. Leaving Mr Baldwin to guard over the body, he raced to a public telephone box located in Church Street to raise the alarm.

Inspector Philip Plumbley, stationed at Darlaston, arrived on the scene at 10.15 p.m., just as it began to rain. The body lay some 160yds from the nearest street lamp in Queen Street and he used the light of a hand-held torch to examine the immediate area. The unfortunate woman was clothed in a brown overcoat, light green working overall, green pullover, brown corduroy skirt, nylon stockings and black suede bootees. On her head she wore a floral-patterned cotton scarf. Her lower clothing had been torn and pulled up over her waist leaving intimate areas of her body exposed, which had been covered with a gents raincoat upon discovery. The police officer observed two small but distinct abrasions to the left side of her nose and the woman's mouth was open. Nearby, on the right hand side of the rough path facing Arden Place, he found a dog lead, a brown paper bag containing the recently purchased wool and knitting pattern, and also a pair of green woollen gloves. Between these items and the body was a discarded piece of an overcoat belt and a copy of a magazine called *Secrets*! These two items lay in a deep depression in the ground.

Home Office Pathologist, Professor J.M. Webster, made a preliminary examination of the body (as found) at 1 a.m. the following morning. Allowing for the very cold night and the condition and stiffness of the corpse, he formed the opinion that the victim had met her death between 5 p.m. and 6 p.m. the previous evening. The position of the body was such as would have resulted in death either before, during or after sexual intercourse had taken place, suggesting an attack of rape by an unknown assailant. Another motive to be investigated was that of robbery, her purse containing the six shilling postal order being found to be missing.

A full post-mortem was carried out by Professor Webster at 2 a.m., when it was determined that foul play had taken place. In his opinion, the cause of death was asphyxia resulting from pressure of an unknown assailant's hand over the victim's nose and mouth, probably done so as to stifle her screams. In this knowledge, a manhunt was launched as police activity continued at the murder scene throughout the night.

Later in the day, a press conference was held at Wednesbury police station at which Superintendent H.J. Brookes appealed for witnesses to come forward who may have seen Lilian Collins any time after she left Miss French's shop and the post office prior to the discovery of her body. In the evening, police set up a mobile incident unit at the junction of Church Street with Queen Street, and began to stop and question passers-by. This proved very useful, with one positive sighting of Mrs Collins reported by her next-door neighbour, Mrs Minnie Brownhill, who stated that whilst she was walking up Queen Street towards the shops at 5.30 p.m. with her two children, Mrs Collins passed in the opposite direction, walking down the middle of the road, before crossing to the right in the direction of the wasteland.

Those stopped were also asked by the police whether they had observed anyone loitering in the area the previous evening. Of interest to the investigation team, three independent witnesses gave the same name and description of a young local man, Kenneth Causer, a nineteen-year-old national serviceman on leave from Chester Barracks to which he had already begun the return journey. He had been staying at his parents' house in Queen Street, situated right opposite the wasteland, affording an uninterrupted view across to the victim's home.

On Friday morning, 3 December, a shocked Raymond Collins, now a widower after less than four months' marriage, arrived at Wolverhampton railway station from Scotland and was driven by private car to Moxley. When asked for comment by waiting reporters, he replied simply, 'I feel too sick and too stunned to speak about it.' As he joined his grieving mother and sisters-in-law at Arden Place, the police continued to comb the nearby wasteland, raking and cutting the grass around the spot where his short-lived wife had met her doom. The next day, an inquest was opened at Wednesbury, but adjourned until the following Friday.

Later that day, Saturday 4 December, a thirteen-year-old schoolboy, Raymond John Horton from Bull Lane, Moxley, approached a police constable with a purse he found hidden behind the front boundary wall of the Wesleyan chapel in the High Street, adjacent to the Bilston bound bus stop. It was identified as the missing property belonging to Lilian Collins. Inside were three scraps of paper, a sixpence, some pills and some machine drill bits. Gone was the 6s postal order purchased the previous Wednesday.

Acting upon a request from Staffordshire Police, Detective Constable John Derek Hill of Chester Constabulary visited the Army camp where Kenneth Causer was serving as a private in the Royal Catering Corps. In the presence of two Army officers, the detective explained to Causer that he was checking on the movements of people in the vicinity of Queen Street and Arden Place, Moxley, on the evening of Wednesday 1 December 1954, and had reason to believe that he had been seen there. Causer confirmed that he had been in his home district on forty-eight hours' leave from service.

When asked by Detective Constable Hill if he could give a detailed account of his whereabouts at that time, Causer replied, 'Yes. Is this in connection with that woman who was found. I read about it in the newspapers.' He made a statement, which he checked and signed, alleging that on the afternoon of 1 December, he visited his grandfather in Darlaston, staying to watch the international football match on television. Later, he returned home to Queen Street for tea and then left at about 5.30 p.m., heading for the Odeon Cinema at Bilston, where he arrived at 6 p.m.

This was relayed back to Staffordshire Police, who despatched Detective Inspector William Gray to make further inquiries. He arrived at Chester Barracks on Tuesday 7 December when, in interview, he said to Causer 'I am making enquiries about the death of Mrs Lilian Collins and would like a word with you at the police station.' Causer replied 'All right, I'll come with you but can I change first?' He changed into civilian clothing and accompanied Inspector Gray to Chester police station.

Once there, the inspector asked Causer to again give an account of his movements. Causer said:

> I have told a policeman at the Army camp, but if you know the district, I can explain better to you. On 1 December, I was late in getting up. I left the house just before 2.30 p.m. to watch the match at my grandfather's. I saw the whole of the second half. I left at 4 p.m. and got home ten minutes later and had my tea. I then read comics and books before catching the bus to see *Romeo and Juliet* at the Odeon.

When asked, Causer denied that he had stopped on the way. Pressed by the Inspector with the same question, he affirmed, 'I'm sure.'

Inspector Gray then put it to him, 'I have reason to believe you were seen at the top of Queen Street at 6.15 p.m.' Causer replied, 'Whoever has told you that is wrong. I was in the picture house then.' The inspector then asked Causer if he knew Miss Florence Freeman of Queen Street and he replied that he did, stating that he saw her that evening whilst on his way to the Odeon. 'Miss Freeman doesn't leave her workplace in Bilston until 6 p.m.,', said the Inspector, 'therefore it must have been sometime after 6 p.m. when you say you saw her!' Causer fell silent. 'Were you at the top of Queen Street at 6.15 p.m.?', Causer was asked. He paused a while before replying, 'Yes.' Next, the inspector asked him to account for his movements between 5.15 p.m. and 6.15 p.m. Causer knew he was cornered. After a further lengthy pause, he suddenly blurted out, 'I did not intend to kill her, believe me.' The inspector cautioned Causer before asking, 'What did you intend to do?' Causer's reply was, 'I only wanted to make love with her, but she fainted when we were on the grass. I got frightened and ran off. I thought that she would come round.' He denied taking the unfortunate woman's purse.

Inspector Gray then took a statement from Causer, in which he dictated:

I was standing on the corner of Queen Street when I saw Mrs Collins cross towards the wasteland. I thought I would try to make love to her. We were lying on the ground when I realised that she had fainted. I put my hand over her mouth to stop her from screaming. I dragged her towards the wall and left her there because I was frightened, but did not think she was dead. I did not murder her. I returned home and later went to the cinema.

Causer was arrested and conveyed back to the Black Country.

At 11 p.m. the same day, Inspector Philip Plumbley cautioned Causer at Wednesbury police station before charging him with the murder of Lilian Joan Collins. The prisoner then elected to give the following statement:

I had no intention of killing her. I was standing on the corner when she came from the Wednesbury direction. She crossed over towards the path and I knew her a bit. I followed her and caught up with her. I put my arm on her shoulders but I slipped into a hole and pulled her with me. I started to make love to her by kissing her. We were both lying on the grass when I realised she had fainted. I put my hand over her mouth to stop her from screaming. I left her because I was frightened but I did not think she was dead.

The day after, Causer requested to see Detective Inspector William Gray in the presence of his solicitor, Mr Sydney W. Smith and told him:

You asked me about a purse yesterday. I did take the purse and removed 5s 6d from it. There was also a 6s postal order which I took and exchanged at the Army camp.

*Church Street, Moxley, with the High Street beyond, c. 1954. Kenneth Causer waited for his victim at the corner of Queen Street, located between the telephone box and Downs' butcher's van. (Author's collection)*

I threw the purse over the wall by the bus stop at Moxley. It dropped on the grass when we fell together and I picked it up. That is the whole truth now.

Mourners braved the first snow of winter as the funeral cortège assembled in Arden Place, witnessed by friends and neighbours of Lilian Collins, standing in silent groups. The hearse was preceded by a police car in which sat Superintendent T.H. Gregory of Bilston police. So was the scene on Wednesday 8 December, one week to the day since the terrible tragedy. The cortège slowly made its way to All Saints' Church, Moxley, passing the Queen Street home of the accused as it progressed. Stoker Raymond Collins RN walked immediately behind his wife's coffin, which bore his wreath of a floral anchor with a card enscribed ''Til we meet again', followed by the principal mourners, including the victim's six broken-hearted sisters. The service was conducted by the Revd Thomas Grimsdale Kelsey, watched by a congregation of about 120, mostly women wearing winter headscarves. Many were colleagues of the dead woman from the Rubery Owen & Co. Ltd factory, almost opposite the church. Internment took place at Bilston Cemetery, the biting wind and driving snow keeping sightseers to a minimum. During the 2-mile journey from Moxley through lunch hour traffic, workers hurrying home to their midday meal stopped briefly along the main road to watch and pay their last respects.

*High Street, Moxley, showing the bus stop where Kenneth Causer discarded Lilian Joan Collins' purse behind the Wesleyan chapel forecourt wall. The trolley bus is passing the entrance to Queen Street. (Courtesy of J.C. Brown)*

Causer attended the resumed inquest on Friday 10 December when he heard Professor J.M. Webster, Home Office Pathologist, detail his results of a post-mortem he carried out upon the body of Lilian Collins to the coroner, Mr Frank Cooper. He explained that when he examined the body at 2 a.m. on Thursday 2 December, it was fully clothed, although there was much tearing of the intimate garments and much violence had been used to do so. Although Mrs Collins was a healthy woman, she was frail in physique and was not the type who could put up a struggle against a muscular opponent. Death was due to shock and asphyxia due to closure of the external respiratory orifices during rape or attempted rape.

Also that day, Causer made a two-minute appearance in the dock before Mr Harry Parkes JP and was remanded in custody until the following Friday. His solicitor, Mr Smith, indicated that on that day, he would apply for counsel to be assigned to the defence owing to the seriousness of the charge.

At the committal hearing held on Wednesday 26 January 1955, lasting five hours, evidence was given of the three independent sightings made of Causer in the vicinity of the crime on the evening of Wednesday 1 December the previous year.

The first witness was Mrs Elizabeth Freeman, from Queen Street, who together with Joyce Collett, had accompanied Lilian Collins into the centre of Moxley that fateful day after leaving their workplace in Holyhead Road. At 5.20 p.m., only five minutes after parting company with her two colleagues, she walked back up Queen Street to purchase some cakes from a grocer's in Church Street, passing Kenneth Causer as she did so. He was standing on the corner of the two streets and was still at the same spot when she returned home with her purchase a few minutes later.

Nearly an hour afterwards, Causer was seen at the top of Queen Street at 6.15 p.m. by fourteen-year-old schoolboy, Brian Harrison, whilst walking in the direction of his home, which was in close proximity to that of Causer's.

The third, and most critical sighting, was made by Miss Florence Freeman, another Queen Street resident, who alighted from the Wednesbury-bound bus at 6.15 p.m., having earlier finished work in Bilston. She also remembered seeing Brian Harrison walking home, corroborating the exact time that the schoolboy had given and making it impossible for Causer to have been at the Odeon Cinema in Bilston as he had stated to police detectives at Chester before confessing.

Causer was placed on trial at Stafford Assizes on Wednesday 9 March 1955 before His Lordship, Mr Justice Devlin. Prosecuting for the Crown were Mr John Busse QC and Mr W. Field Hunt. The defence was led by Mr Douglas Draycott, on the instructions of Mr Sydney W. Smith, solicitor. Causer pleaded 'not guilty' and reserved his defence.

*The Odeon Cinema, Bilston. (Author's collection)*

Witness for the prosecution, Home Office Pathologist Professor J.M. Webster, told of arriving at the crime scene at 1 a.m. on Thursday 2 December 1954 and later holding a post-mortem examination of the victim's body. In cross-examination by the defence, Mr Draycott asked, 'Did all the evidence point to a very rapid death?' Professor Webster replied, 'Yes Sir, sixty to 120 seconds from the time the air was cut off.' Mr Draycott then suggested, 'There was evidence, was there not, of chronic disease of the heart?'

'No', replied the professor, 'The heart was in good condition.'

'Any disease of the lung?' continued Mr Draycott, to which the reply was, 'No, I especially looked for that.'

Eager to acquit his client, Mr Draycott then asked if there was any evidence the victim was suffering from bronchitis. Professor Webster said that there was none. 'Physically she was below normal?' urged Mr Draycott. The professor replied, 'In my opinion, this woman was suffering from some wasting condition of the muscles. She would not be able to put up much resistance to violence because of her poor physical condition.' Quickly, Mr Draycott asked, 'Apart from the scratches and the torn clothing, was there any evidence of violence?'

'No,' answered the professor, 'although considerable violence had been used to tear the clothing.'

Another witness, Private John Richard Kyffin from Dingley, Liverpool, serving in the Royal Army Catering Corps at the same barracks as Causer recalled the evening when the accused returned back from leave. He handed Private Kyffin a postal order for 6s and asked if he would cash it on his behalf. This he did, handing the money over to Causer the next day.

In his summing up, Mr Justice Devlin told the jury, 'If rape was intended, the defendant would be guilty of murder. However, if rape was not intended, the verdict would have to be one of manslaughter.' After retiring for seventy-five minutes, the foreman of the jury indicated that they agreed with the former of the two verdicts suggested by the judge, finding Kenneth Causer 'guilty of murder', but adding a strong recommendation for mercy.

As he passed the sentence of death upon Causer, the judge said that he would convey the jury's recommendation to the Home Secretary, which fortunately for the young killer was accepted, his sentence being reduced to one of penal servitude.

# 10

# THE WOMAN OF MANY COLOURS

*Tipton, 1958*

With an impressive thirteen miles of canals within its parish boundaries, Tipton proudly proclaims to be the 'Venice of the Midlands'. Such is the extent of the inland waterways network in the town, that to access its main centre from any direction, a canal must be crossed. The reason for the proliferation of these eighteenth-century navigations was the town's many and varied ironworks and collieries, which were as equally well served by the nineteenth-century railway companies, sometimes merging together to form canal and rail interchanges.

A typical example was Bloomfield Basin, a triangular-shaped complex approached from Bloomfield Road, via Bloomfield Terrace, beneath the embankment of the Oxford, Worcester and Wolverhampton Line of the Great Western Railway. Its other two sides were bounded by the Stour Valley Line of the London and North Western Railway, and the Wolverhampton Level of the Birmingham Canal. The three basins, where freight was once transferred from barge to wagon, are now filled in and the site today is operated by the Bloomfield Recycling Co.

In 1958, this was the base of Rhodes Iron & Steel Stockholders Ltd, where, at 8.30 a.m. on Tuesday 18 February, Mr Albert W.R. Wright, the stockyard foreman, and Mr Joseph Henry Fisher, a mobile crane driver, ventured out into the cold morning air to measure up some steel girders. They had measured only three lengths when, behind a stack of girders, they discovered the body of a woman lying prostrate on the open ground, with visible head injuries and evidence of having been sexually interfered with. At once, they returned to the office and alerted the local police, with Detective Sergeant H.I. Simmonds arriving at the yard a few minutes later. In a short time, he was joined by the head of Staffordshire

*The former entrance to Rhodes Iron & Steel Stockholders, approached from Bloomfield Terrace, Tipton. (Author's collection)*

CID, Detective Superintendent Frank Tucker. They found the location of the body to be quite isolated; although the nearest houses were 50yds away in Bloomfield Terrace and Lilac Avenue, they were separated from the stockyard by the steep railway embankment.

Death was undoubtedly due to violence. The woman was white-skinned, but with a sallow complexion, and had a protruding upper jaw with badly rotted teeth. She was of a slight build, weighing about 7 stones, and appeared to be aged between thirty-five and forty years. Her face bore evidence of having been badly beaten up. She lay on her back, with the lower half of her body twisted to the left. Her right leg was crossed over the left leg. Her right arm was pinned under her back whilst her left arm rested alongside the left side of her body, the left hand being gloved.

Curiously, she was dressed in a multitude of vividly coloured clothes, her unconventional dress-sense later proving helpful in identifying the body. These consisted of a green overcoat, which was opened at the neck, a grey woollen jacket, yellow cardigan, red smock, pink skirt, green and white apron, thick brown cotton lisle stockings, secured with elastic garters, and a brand new pair of brown leather shoes. Her upper clothing had been raised, exposing her thighs, and her stockings turned down to just below the knees. The woman's head was bare, although her hair was tied with a bright red ribbon. A yellow button from her cardigan lay alongside, and a bloodstained handkerchief was recovered from the stack of girders.

Nearby, in a small depression in the ground, Detective Sergeant Simmonds found a screw-type bottle cap, together with two pieces of cellophane, one red and one yellow. From where the body lay, the two policemen traced a pair of parallel drag marks for a distance of 92ft 6in over the rough ground, to a boundary fence at the bottom of the railway embankment. The marks terminated at a concrete fence post, from which a piece of cement was freshly broken. Three feet away was found a brown felt ladies hat.

When the body was examined, it was seen that she had suffered a severe blow to the back of the head, either from coming into contact with the damaged concrete fence post, or possibly the result of a fall onto a hard surface. On the fingers of her right hand, she was found to be wearing two costume rings, one silver and the other marcasite.

Later in the day, the unfortunate victim was identified when woman Police Constable A. Ross matched her description to a woman arrested nine weeks earlier on a petty shoplifting charge in Dudley town centre. Her name was Lilian May Cox, a thirty-nine-year-old spinster, who lived with her sister and eighty-year-old widowed mother, Mrs Emma Cox, in Harrold Road, Blackheath. They told the police that she had left the house at about 2.30 p.m. the previous afternoon without saying where she was going. When she failed to return home by bedtime, they presumed she had visited friends and stayed the night.

In September 1957, her sister had told her to leave the family home because she had begun staying out at night. For a time, she slept rough in the quarrying district of Rowley Regis, sometimes bedding down in a small hut on the slopes of Dudley Golf Course. At the beginning of November, she obtained lodgings with Mrs Irene Rudd and her husband, who, with their two children, lived at Perry's

*Dudley's ancient castle, guarding over the town. (Courtesy of Bernard Minton)*

Lake, Springfield Lane, Rowley Regis. Mr Rudd, a chemical process worker, had known Miss Cox for twenty years. Following arrest for involvement in the theft of some Christmas decorations at the Dudley branch of Woolworths, she appeared in court on 23 December and was placed on probation for two years. Afterwards, she returned to live with her mother and sister and was never seen by the Rudd's again.

In the days following the discovery of her body, Mrs Rudd told a local newspaper reporter, 'Shortly before Christmas, Lilian left the house about 7 p.m. one evening. I popped out to fetch some groceries, and saw her flash a torch three times. Then a plain green van pulled up and she got in, before it drove away. I have not seen the van since and she never mentioned the name of the driver.' Mrs Rudd never got the impression that there was any one man in particular in Miss Cox's life, although she did carry a photograph in her handbag. She had spoken of her 'boyfriend in Dudley to whom she was soon to be married'. 'She was talking about her boyfriends all the time', said Mrs Rudd, adding, 'Whether she was just bragging or not, we do not know.'

She was well known in the Blackeath district for her love of brightly coloured clothing, her favourites being a scarlet or striking green sweater worn with brown slacks. She frequented many public houses in the vicinity and was passionately fond of the movies, visiting the local cinemas almost on a daily basis for a matinée or early evening screening. It was established that on Thursday 13 February, she had visited the Odeon Cinema, Castle Hill, Dudley, to see the film *Les Girls*, shortly after leaving Dudley bus station at 3 p.m. She left the cinema alone at 6.20 p.m. The police put out an appeal for cinema goers who may have seen Miss Cox to get in touch with them. Officers also visited public houses, milk bars and cafés in Blackheath, Rowley Regis, Dudley and Tipton, in an effort to trace the woman's last movements, and to find out who her friends and associates were.

Enquiries revealed that Miss Cox had been doing casual domestic work in the Rowley Regis area, but other than this, no significant information had been received by the investigators on that first day. Late in the afternoon, Colonel G.W.R. Hearn, the Chief Constable of Staffordshire, arrived in Tipton to take charge of the murder investigation.

In the evening, a post-mortem examination of the body was carried out by Home Office Pathologist, Dr F.E.D. Griffiths. The autopsy revealed that Lilian Cox had been the victim of a brutal assault, during which she was battered about the head, resulting in her upper jaw being fractured in two places. Injuries to her chin and face were probably caused by being hit with her assailant's fist. There was a severe contusion to the rear of the scalp, underneath which the skull had been fractured. Certain injuries could have been caused by natural or unnatural intercourse. She had undoubtedly been sexually interfered with. There were no visible defence injuries on the hands or the arms, suggesting that the blow to the skull had first rendered her unconscious. Death, though, was due to manual strangulation. Dr Griffiths believed that no weapons had been used in the vicious attack. The killer had beaten and strangled her with his own bare hands. He concluded that death had taken place about 10.30 p.m. the previous Monday night.

The following day, Colonel Hearn called in assistance from Scotland Yard's murder squad, with Detective Superintendent John MacIver and Detective Sergeant John O'Connell travelling up from London to the Black Country to oversee enquiries. At a press conference, Detective Superintendent McIver told reporters, 'From when she left home until the body was discovered, the woman seems to have vanished into thin air.' He revealed that an empty miniature rum bottle had been found 28ft from the concrete post, where it was believed Miss Cox had been attacked. Also, the police were searching for her purse which they had reason to believe she had been carrying with her when she left home. Detective Superintendent MacIver appealed to the public, 'We are still anxious to find the woman's small brown leather purse, measuring 4½in by 2½in, with a zip fastener across the top.'

Superintendent Frank Tucker added, 'Miss Cox was only very frail and could have been overpowered by any normal man. There is evidence of manual injuries to the throat and head. This woman had been badly beaten up and no other instrument was used.' Together, the two policemen again urged members of the public to come forward with any information if they had seen Lilian Cox in Blackheath, Dudley or Tipton on the Monday afternoon or evening.

The appeal proved most successful, with two very important leads being received almost immediately. A woman visiting the Odeon Cinema in Dudley on the Monday evening recalled seeing Miss Cox sitting in the auditorium with a man who was exhibiting an annoying behaviour and had unruly hair hanging over his forehead.

*The former Odeon Cinema, Castle Hill, Dudley. (Author's collection)*

She had often seen the woman with protruding dirty teeth in the cinema and matched her to the description given out by the press. Notably, she wore a bright red ribbon in her hair that evening.

The other lead came from staff at the Fountain Inn, Tipton, famously associated with William Perry, the 'Tipton Slasher' – not some Black Country 'Jack the Ripper', but the Bare Knuckle Boxing Champion of England from 1850 to 1857. They too had seen Miss Cox with a man of similar description, who had purchased, amongst other items, a miniature bottle of rum to take away from the premises on the same Monday evening. More so, on leaving the public house, the couple turned into Factory Road alongside, and walked in the direction of Bloomfield Basin.

From the description of Miss Cox's companion, a thirty-year-old bachelor was interviewed later that day. George Smith, a refuse collector living in Longbank Road, Oakham, Dudley, made a statement admitting that he had been in the Odeon on Monday evening, but insisted that he had seen Miss Cox sitting with another man. Without any strong evidence against him, Mr Smith was released by the police without charge.

On Thursday 20 February, the stack of girders at Bloomfield Basin, near to where the body was found, were removed and the ground beneath carefully searched. This produced the missing cork from the empty rum bottle, which by now was being examined for fingerprints by forensic scientists. Members of the Midland Crime Squad could be seen combing the Great Western Railway embankment with garden rakes in their continued search for the victim's missing leather purse.

*The Fountain Inn, Owen Street, Tipton, with entrance to Factory Road seen left. (Author's collection)*

*Canal towpath at the rear of the Fountain Inn, where Lilian May Cox walked to her death with George Smith. (Author's collection)*

Officers were instructed to meticulously search every inch of the stockyard over again. Superintendent Tucker informed the press, 'Several people have already come forward with information, which officers are at present sifting through.' The newspapers, in turn, printed reports of factory girls afraid to walk to work alone whilst a killer was on the loose in their midst.

The funeral of Lilian Cox, unlike the media circus surrounding her death, was a very private affair, with only family mourners present when her body was laid to rest at Oldbury Cemetery, on Wednesday 26 February. A police officer on duty there told a pressman, 'We are only here to see that Miss Cox gets a decent burial'. This might have been a hint that they were no longer searching for a suspect, the police tradition of plain clothes detectives mingling with mourners and sightseers not being observed. There were eight wreaths left around the graveside, one of which was simply worded, 'From a good friend'.

That night, in a surprise move, George Smith was brought back to Tipton police station for further questioning. Interviewed by Detective Superintendents MacIver and Tucker, he was asked to account for his movements on the evening of Monday 17 February, once he had left the Odeon Cinema in Dudley. After first sticking to his original statement, that he saw Miss Cox with another man, he was informed that witnesses had come forward who had seen them both together, not just there, but at the Fountain Inn too.

Smith then admitted that they had sat alongside one another, saying, 'Miss Cox was a bad woman. She kept coming beside me and I kept pushing her away. Some boys had been shooting peas at her, so she asked me to take her outside.' Detective Superintendent MacIver urged Smith to continue with his account. 'I agreed to go outside with her, and she asked me to walk her along', said Smith, adding, 'We just continued walking.'

'Where did you walk to?' enquired the officer.

Smith guilefully replied, 'I cannot remember anything after that until I remember catching the bus back home in Dudley. I must have had a blackout.'

Detective Superintendent Tucker now regarded him with some suspicion and intervened, suggesting to Smith that it would be favourable for himself to be more helpful with his answers. Smith's memory made a remarkable improvement. He told of going to the Fountain Inn at Tipton and buying several bottles of alcohol. They walked along Factory Road, stopping for a drink by the canal on the way. 'I didn't do anything to the woman', insisted Smith.

Detective Superintendent MacIver informed Smith it was likely he would be arrested for murder. He then opened up, declaring, 'The trouble between Miss Cox and myself was because she accused me of making her pregnant. I remember it all now. I was standing against the fence. She said that I put a baby into her, and I never did. I hit her hard in the mouth with my fist.' He then described how he laid her on the ground and committed the sexual assault, ending, 'I left her lying by the irons in the stockyard. I lost my head.'

The interview had crossed into the following day. At 1.15 a.m. on Thursday 27 February, George Smith was officially cautioned and then charged with the murder of Lilian May Cox. Detective Sergeant Simmonds took possession of all the clothes Smith was wearing, and parcelled them up for forensic examination. A special court was scheduled for midday.

Prior to this, at 10.55 a.m., Smith was having his fingerprints taken by Detective Sergeant Simmonds in the CID office at Tipton Central police station, in Lower Church Lane, when he suddenly said to the officer, 'I am very sorry about this. If you take me to the place, I will show you what happened.' Detective Sergeant Simmonds finished taking the prisoner's prints before informing Detective Superintendent MacIver of what he had said. There was still an hour to pass before Smith's court appearance, so it was decided that he should be taken back to the stockyard, in the custody of Detective Inspector P. Minshall, of Willenhall.

Alighting from the detective's car at the stockyard, Smith looked across the ground between the entrance drive and the canal, declaring, 'Yes, this is the place.' He walked back to the railway bridge, at the end of Bloomfield Terrace, and pointing to the wall, said, 'That's where we stood.' He then pointed to the canal towpath, leading to Bloomfield Road, and said, 'We came down along here.' Walking to the wire fence separating the railway embankment from the stockyard, he pointed to a low stone wall, saying, 'We had some drinks there.' Smith then walked diagonally across the stockyard towards a pile of bricks. On the way, he pointed towards the wire fence, and said, 'We had more drinks there.' Almost immediately afterwards, he pointed towards where the stack of girders had recently been moved, and acknowledged, 'That's where you found her.' He continued to walk towards the pile of bricks, which he examined. Then he moved to an adjacent stack of sheet steel and looked about on the ground. He picked up a clear broken bottle, smelt it and said, 'No, that's not the bottle.' Detective Inspector Minshall then drove him back to the police station.

At midday, Smith appeared before Councillor James Edmond Salter JP, the only magistrate present, at a Tipton Police Court Special Hearing. The Magistrate's Clerk was Mr Frank Brown, assisted by Mr Harry Shepherd. Smith, dressed in a dirty grey sports jacket, open neck shirt, blue trousers and dirty shoes, stood in the dock between Police Constables K.B. Bennett and D. Russell. He was not handcuffed.

Detective Superintendent Tucker said that at 10.15 p.m. the previous night, he and Detective Superintendent MacIver of Scotland Yard, interviewed the prisoner and took various statements, as a result of which, Smith was charged with the murder of Lilian May Cox on Monday 17 February. When asked if he wished to reply to the charge, Smith replied, 'No, Sir. I've said my statement. I'm sorry.' Superintendent L. Pullman, head of Wednesbury Police Division, said that the matter would have to be placed in the hands of the Director of Public Prosecutions, which in so doing would take about three weeks. Mr Brown asked Smith if he had anything to say on the matter, to which he replied, 'No, Sir.'

Superintendent Pullman then said that the question of legal aid had been explained to the prisoner, but he did not seem to appreciate it. Mr Brown asked Smith, 'Do you wish to be represented by a solicitor when the prosecution is in a position to proceed?' Smith replied, 'Yes, Sir.' Asked by Mr Brown how much he earned per week, Smith answered, '£12 odd.' When it became clear that Smith had no savings to pay for his defence, Councillor Salter announced that legal aid would be granted. He then remanded the prisoner in custody to reappear at Tipton Magistrates Court the following Tuesday. The hearing had lasted just eleven minutes.

Dudley solicitor, Mr Brian Dutfield, was appointed to represent Smith, when he faced the said court on Tuesday 4 March, in an even shorter hearing of only three minutes duration. The clerk, Mr Frank Brown, asked if the evidence of arrest needed to be repeated, but this was declined. Superintendent Pullman successfully applied for a second remand, explaining that police enquiries were still incomplete, and that the facts of the case had not yet been reported to the Director of Public Prosecutions.

Smith was remanded on a further two occasions. On Tuesday 11 March, Mr Dutfield made no objection when Superintendent Pullman applied for the third custodial order, confirming that the Director of Public Prosecutions was not in receipt of the facts, and it was actually not possible for the case to proceed. The final remand was made on Tuesday 18 March, on which occasion, Superintendent Pullman said information had arrived from the Director of Public Prosecutions, that it would be possible for the summary hearing to be held the following Monday.

Mr Dutfield protested that the counsel engaged to conduct the defence would not be available on that day. He had informed the clerk of Tipton Court of this, and asked for an alternative date to be fixed. He pointed out that it was likely the case would eventually be put before Staffordshire Assizes, which were not being held until the beginning of July. After consulting with the clerk, Mr Frank Brown, the Chairman of the Bench, Mr H.H. Taylor JP, told the solicitor, 'I am very sorry, but the case will have to go forward next Monday at 3 p.m.'

'If that is your decision, then I must abide by it.' Mr Dutfield replied.

The inquest into the death of Lilian May Cox was held early in the afternoon of Monday 24 March, only hours before Smith's scheduled court appearance. The coroner heard from Dr F.E.D. Griffiths, who had carried out the autopsy on the victim's body, that death from manual strangulation had occurred, after the woman had been subjected to a sexual assault, whilst lying unconscious. Mr Peter George William Cobb, chemist, said that after he examined a blood specimen, he found that the woman had consumed the equivalent of one pint of beer, or one and an half fluid ounces of spirits, shortly before death.

Some revealing information came from Mr Brian Robert Morgan, staff biologist at the West Midlands Forensic Science Laboratory. He had examined Miss Cox's shoes and found the toes to be scraped, and the welts filled with loose dirt. This, he suggested, was because she had been dragged across the stockyard face downwards to the place her body was found. The inquest was afterwards adjourned until 1 August.

Later the same Monday afternoon, at Tipton Magistrates Court, the summary hearing began. It was afterwards adjourned until the following day, when committal was made, lasting in total a lengthy eight hours. The Director of Public Prosecutions was represented by Mr E.C. MacDermott, whilst the defence was conducted by Mr Douglas Draycott.

On the Monday, evidence was heard from witnesses who were present at the Odeon Cinema, Castle Hill, Dudley, on the evening of Monday 17 February. The cinema, now a Jehova's Witness Kingdom Hall, stood opposite the entrance to the town's famous zoo, in its ancient castle setting, both opened in 1937.

Mrs Sophia May Mills, of Corporation Road, Dudley, said that she arrived at the Odeon about 5.50 p.m., accompanied by her two nieces. They sat in the 2s seats in the left block, about six rows back from the screen. A man and woman were sitting in the same row, about three or four seats away. 'I had seen the same woman several times before in the cinema, and a few times in town', said Mrs Mills. She had also seen the man two or three times before, sitting with the woman in the cinema. She described the woman as very ordinary looking with big, dirty teeth. She was wearing a bright red ribbon in her hair.

After Mrs Mills had watched the film for a time, she was distracted by some boys sat in front of her who were shooting dried peas at the couple. She looked across the row and saw that the man and woman were loving each other. The woman had her arms partly around the man and he was in the same position. She shouted to the couple to behave themselves, but they took no notice. The boys continued to shoot peas. Embarrassed for her nieces, Mrs Mills called out, 'I wish you would stop it, if you don't stop, I shall fetch the manager to you.' At this, the couple stood up and left the auditorium. The time was about 7.45 p.m. Asked by Mr MacDermott whether she could see the man in court, Mrs Mills walked up to Smith, who was sitting in the dock between two policemen, and said, 'This is the man.'

Her niece, fifteen-year-old Hazel Madeleine Williams, of Cypress Road, Dudley, told of seeing the woman lying across the man's lap. 'My aunt spoke to them, and twenty minutes later they left through the exit at the side of the screen.' she said. The other girl, June Ann Simcox, aged fourteen, of Corporation Road, Dudley, said that the man went out first and the woman followed seconds later. The woman had almost got to the exit, when she returned to where she had been sitting and picked something up from off the floor, then went out again. Miss Simcox said she recognised the woman as someone she had seen there before because of her protruding teeth in the upper jaw.

David Peter Cookson, a thirteen-year-old schoolboy of Pitman Street, Kates Hill, Dudley, said that he was sitting in the 2s seats with a friend, when they saw a man and woman behind them, kissing. 'I had a pea shooter with me and my friend and I fired peas at them', he said. Handed a photograph of Miss Cox, he said, 'Yes, that is the woman.'

Mrs Ethel Markham, wife of the licensee of the Fountain Inn, Owen Street, Tipton, described serving a man with half a bottle of port, a miniature bottle of rum, and two half pint bottles of brown ale, on the same Monday night. The man was with a woman, who she later identified as Miss Cox. A barmaid at the inn, Mrs Mary Ellen Marsh, of Union Street, Tipton, said that at 8.30 p.m., she saw the couple leave the premises and walk along Factory Road, alongside. She had not seen either of them before.

Detective Sergeant Simmonds told of retracing, on foot, the pair's journey from Dudley to Tipton. From the Odeon to the Fountain Inn was a distance of 1 mile and 350yds. He had walked it slowly and it took him twenty-seven minutes. From the Fountain Inn to the stockyard, it was 1,232yds, and took fourteen minutes to complete.

Mr Leslie Derek Smith, brother of the accused, said that he saw him board a bus for home, on the opposite side of the road from the Odeon, at 10.30 p.m. that night. Cross-examined by Mr Draycott, he agreed that his brother could not read or write. He also agreed that it would be right to describe him as 'backwards'. His brother was a person who preferred going out with male friends and he had never seen him in the company of a woman. 'He was not the sort to pick up a prostitute.' he said, adding, 'He seemed perfectly normal when he got on the bus. He was in no way worried or agitated.'

Foreman at Rhodes Iron & Steel Stockholders Ltd, Bloomfield Basin, Tipton, Mr Albert Wright, and mobile crane driver, Mr Joseph Henry Fisher, both described jointly finding Miss Cox's battered and strangled body at 8.30 a.m. on the chilly morning of Tuesday 18 February, Mr Fisher saying, 'I had measured only three lengths of steel, when I saw a woman's body.'

*The former Rhodes Iron & Steel Stockholders Ltd, seen from the railway embankment. Note the concrete fence posts, seen to the right. (Author's collection)*

At the close of the hearing, Smith was committed for trial at Staffordshire Summer Assizes, his case being heard on Tuesday 8 July. On this occasion, prosecuting for the Crown were Mr Ryder-Richardson with Mr Francis Barnes. Mr Douglas Draycott again represented the prisoner, assisted by Mr R.G. Micklethwait. Smith wore a blue shirt, open at the neck, and a check sports jacket.

Mr Ryder-Richardson told the jury that a post-mortem examination had revealed that Miss Cox had received a blow to the face which fractured her jaw in two places. She had also suffered a blow to the back of her head, fracturing her skull. 'She was criminally assaulted, and met her death by manual strangulation.' he said. Informing them of her movements the night before her body was discovered, he continued, 'She was seen in the Odeon Cinema, Dudley, making love with a man, and she later called at the Fountain Inn, Tipton, two thirds of the way between the cinema and the scene of the crime. The man had bought alcohol, which they took away. After she left the public house, she was not seen alive again by anyone except her assailant.'

He told how Smith made a number of statements to the police. He remembered buying alcohol at the Fountain Inn, and walking along Factory Road, at the end of which he accessed the canal, leading into Bloomfield Basin. He first said that he did not do anything unlawful to the woman. The police arrested him for murder, after which he changed his story. He said that the trouble had occurred because she accused him of making her pregnant. He hit her in the mouth with his fist before making sexual connection with her on the ground. 'Here is a case where a woman met her death by violence, and this man has made statements that he was violent towards her at about the time she met her death,' he said.

Detective Sergeant Simmonds, when giving evidence, told Mr Micklethwait, whilst under cross-examination, that Smith had never before been charged with any criminal offence in his life. He knew that Smith had been discharged from National Service in the Army after being declared permanently unfit to serve, on the grounds of being a mental deffective and also suffering from hysteria.

Later, his brother said that he was liable to blackouts, and would burst into tears if shouted at sharply. 'He was not the type who would associate with anyone of an immoral nature', he said, insisting that he was both harmless and inoffensive. Cross-examined, he agreed that whatever happened that night was abnormal conduct for his brother.

Mr Micklethwait, opening the case for the defence, submitted that the evidence so far was that Smith was not in a normal state of mind when the incident occurred. He called three doctors to substantiate this. Dr K.O. Milner of Derby, said that he had formed the opinion that Smith had a permanent abnormality of the mind, suffered since childhood, and was suffering so at the time of the offence. He thought his general level of intelligence was that of a child aged seven or eight years.

Dr P.M. Coates, senior medical officer at Winson Green Prison, Birmingham, said that his opinion, having had Smith under his observation, was that at the time of the events, he was suffering from abnormality of the mind, arising from retarded responsibility. 'I believe it substantially impaired his responsibility for his actions. There was a marked degree of diminished responsibility', he declared. Dr W.A. O'Connor, medical superintendent of a private mental hospital, agreed with Dr Coates, adding that he considered Smith to be a mental defective.

Mr Micklethwait said he would invite the jurors to say that their proper verdict was not one of 'guilty', or 'guilty but insane'. That, he believed, did not come into the matter at all, but the correct verdict would be one of, 'guilty of manslaughter on the grounds of diminished responsibility'. The jury readily agreed, returning the latter verdict, the judge imprisoning Smith for a term of fifteen years.

# BIBLIOGRAPHY

**BOOKS**

Hackwood, Frederick William, *The Annals of Willenhall*, Wolverhampton, 1908.
Hale, Pauline, *Hill Top*, unpublished pamphlet.
Kelly's, *Directory of Staffordshire*, London 1936.
Ludlow, Frederick B., *County Biographies: Staffordshire*, London 1901.

**NEWSPAPERS**

*Dudley Herald*
*Midland Advertiser*
*Midland Chronicle*
*Smethwick Telephone*
*South Staffordshire Times*
*Tipton Herald*
*Walsall Observer*
*Wednesbury Herald*
*Worcestershire County Express*

# INDEX

Other titles published by The History Press

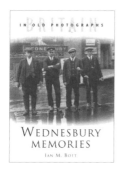

## Wednesbury Memories
IAN M. BOTT

Well-known local author Ian M. Bott recalls halcyon days of neighbourly camaraderie and civic pride in an evocative journey into the history of this ancient Black Country town. He has tracked down over 240 images, many of them previously unpublished, to illustrate bygone streets and buildings, pubs and churches, industry and transport – as well as social events, royal visits and civic occasions.

978 0 7509 3660 6

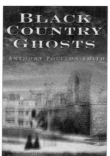

## Black Country Ghosts
ANTHONY POULTON-SMITH

Contained within the pages of this book are strange tales of spectral sightings, active poltergeists and restless spirits appearing in streets, inns, churches, estates, public buildings and private homes across the black country. They include the ghost of a murdered woman in Dudley's Station Hotel cellar, the tragic lovers of Cradley Heath's Haden Estate, Walsall's notorious 'Hand of Glory' and Coseley's enormous black dog forecasting death.

978 0 7509 5044 2

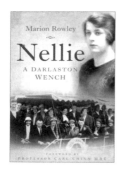

## Nellie A Darlaston Wench
MARION ROWLEY

Nellie White (née Askey) was born in 1906 and brought up in a working-class Darlaston family. Her daughter, Marion Rowley, has compiled this book from memories passed on by Nellie, and the result paints a vivid picture of the Darlaston that has disappeared. Nellie's memories were recorded during her old age, and she recalls in astonishing detail the minutiae of everyday life in this part of the Black Country during the first half of the twentieth century.

978 0 7509 5116 6

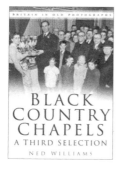

## Black Country Chapels A Third Selection
NED WILLIAMS

For 250 years chapels have been at the heart of Black Country life – both social and religious. Ned Williams has spoken to chapelgoers from a wide range of denominations and has recorded their memories, including Sunday schools, Scouts and Guides, choirs, youth groups, parades and carnivals, outings and sporting events. Richly illustrated, *Black Country Chapels* records a fascinating aspect of the region's history that was at the heart of every community.

978 0 7509 4665 0

Visit our website and discover thousands of other History Press books.

**www.thehistorypress.co.uk**